English Grounds

English Grounds

A Pastoral Journal

Andrew Rumsey

scm press

© Andrew Rumsey 2021

Published in 2021 by SCM Press

Editorial office
3rd Floor, Invicta House,
108–114 Golden Lane,
London EC1Y OTG, UK

www.scmpress.co.uk

SCM Press is an imprint of Hymns Ancient & Modern Ltd
(a registered charity)

Hymns Ancient & Modern® is a registered trademark of
Hymns Ancient & Modern Ltd
13A Hellesdon Park Road,
Norwich,
Norfolk NR6 5DR, UK

ISBN 978-0-334-06114-4

British Library Cataloguing in Publication data
A catalogue record for this book is available
from the British Library

Typeset by Regent Typesetting

Contents

To Grace, Jonah and Tali

From the Savernake

My advice for the storm:
draw close to something rooted,
whose summoning song beckons
with vocation – like an oak
trunk, wrung from
contortions of coping,
which yet baffles the wind.

Acknowledgements

Beginning another book on moving to a new post was not, perhaps, the most sensible commitment to make, although the discipline of completing *English Grounds* has been greatly eased and enabled by the following people, to whom grateful thanks are due. Nick Holtam, for his trust and the instruction: 'I want you to love Wiltshire'; David Shervington at SCM Press for his openness to the idea and readiness to make it happen, and Lynne Archer for her administrative assistance. I greatly appreciated Anthony Wilson, for his cheery encouragement to get writing again; John Inge, for affirming the poetic voice; Ben Quash, for advice when the going was heavy and Colin Heber-Percy, who was going through the same thing. Likewise, I'm grateful to the Groundlings for their enthusiastic support, and to the Friday group at Together for the Common Good, for inspiring conversation on writing days. Thanks also to Stuart Brett for once again assisting so ably with graphic design, Stephen Jeffrey and Daisy Harcourt for their cover ideas, and to Gillian Evans, David Perry and Erica Wagner, who generously read through the draft manuscript and made helpful observations. Finally, my enduring thanks and love to Grace, Jonah and Tali, with whom I have shared each moment of this last, extraordinary season – and to Rebecca, for her endless forbearance with a book-writing husband.

Photographs

Introduction

South by South-West

English Grounds is a small stub of road between London Bridge station and the River Thames, leading to Southwark Crown Court. I came across this appealing name when on jury service some years ago, and it has stayed with me during a time of significant personal transition. Southwark was where my late father began his parish ministry – amid uncleared bombsites and still-cranking dockyards – and where, at the cathedral, I was ordained bishop in 2019. Having spent nearly twenty years 'south of the river' in an Anglican diocese that reaches from Bankside to Gatwick Airport, we moved out to Marlborough in Wiltshire: a pivot point where England teeters away from the capital towards the South West.

I grew up in the 1970s with a patriotic seed sown inside me. Neither my parents nor older brothers shared this affection, nor passed it on, but from early childhood love of country was a strong and abiding bond – an extension of what I felt for home and family. The ghosts of World War Two or bright Beatlemania; British cars and films, customs and companies: all formed my world view and I watched disconsolately ITN's nightly index of manufacturing firms going to the wall, as unemployment graphed towards three million. At our Silver Jubilee street party on the Lewsey Farm estate in Luton, I wore for the fancy dress competition an outfit of fake fur with a rounders bat wrapped in brown paper to wield as a club, and a sign hung from my neck that read 'I am a Great (ancient) Briton'. Second prize won me a snake belt in red, white and blue.

Around the same time, I attended with my grandmother a jumble sale in our church hall, at which she bought me an ancient children's encyclopaedia. On my study book-shelf even now, this contained – among cutaway sections of jet aircraft and instructions on how to crochet – an illus-trated table of dates that quickly imprinted on my memory and kindled an ongoing attachment to British history. To this day, dates remain the only numbers to which I can usefully relate. Geography came later – theology later still – but all of this was about belonging, which is the inarticu-late theme of childhood.

While not quite understanding why, as a vicarage child I was aware that we were somehow both at the centre and the margins of community, with our house a threshold to neighbourhood. The pastoral care modelled to me in those days was at home to humanity: receptive to its untidy demands, as to a divine encounter. And it involved hilari-ous, precarious levels of hospitality. Festive meals for tramps and churchwardens, post-hippy communes turned sour, and our daily adventure of answering the front door, tracing spectral strangers through clouded glass. The thought that Christ might likewise abide – even call upon us unrecognized – implied there was no hard line between heaven and earth, but rather that one was permeable to the other. Church felt like the middle of the village (both real and imagined), yet oddly it also set me apart at school and, in most of the ways that mattered to a youth, made us different.

This was partly at least because, periodically, we moved house. It is one of the paradoxical features of the modern vicar's life that they are so deeply rooted and yet rarely stay put for more than ten years. We moved three times during my childhood (albeit within one diocese), in con-trast to my grandfather, who ministered in a single parish until his death. Whether or not they stay put, being in transit is intrinsic to the Christian's understanding of place, for they are seeking a homeland as yet unseen. It would be fair to say that I am never so fond of places as when travelling between them: leaving one, heading towards another, on the way. Touring the nation by road, in particular, has always seemed to me a mystical business, an impression that even the greyest and most grinding tailback can't quite shake off. This has something to do with summer holidays – a faint sense of promise impressed over long, impatient hours on the A303, an evocative route I now travel daily. Back then we were heading not to work, but for heavenly Devon, in whose light all intermediate stops were transfigured – including, as it happens, sewage farms. My father, who had enjoyed an earlier career in civil engineering, would generously enliven each journey west with (non-negotiable) tours of sewage treatment works whose construction he had overseen during the 1950s. While such detours delayed the seaside *parousia*, they nevertheless succeeded in imbuing even their decomposing fug with top notes of salty expectation.

I mention this background because the way we see places is entirely conditioned by personal narrative. As Continental philosophers were at that time beginning to expound, transitional 'non-places' such as motorways and airports become locations with a unique texture of memory and association once we realize how the dynamics of human movement are bound to the natural environment. The radical geographer Doreen Massey, criticizing the flatness with which most ordinary routes are depicted (not least in the soullessness of satnav space), commented how 'on the road map, you won't drive off the edge of your known world. In space as I want to imagine it, you just might.'

As a child in the back seat, poring over *The Reader's Digest AA Book of the Road*, you almost did. This unsung psalter of British topography featured ingenious flaps that amplified each map to describe (with surprising poetry) the landscape and attractions of the page you were travelling across. It also functioned as a roadside primer, illustrating the wild flowers, fossils and creeping things innumerable to be found on the way. From the overheated queues alongside Stonehenge, it seemed to me that Britain was a teeming playground of curlews, cowslips, coypus and ammonites: an inexhaustible place.

Forty years on, and the need to belong – for 'place' in its fullest sense – is among the most pressing questions in public conversation. Across the globe, the devastation or denial of home is at the heart of geopolitical tension and international migration. Social media – being essentially dislocated – offers connection without context, tending to gather us around a heightened sense of personal identity or caste of opinion. The land is our mediator and uprooted from place, we swiftly become too much for one another. The earthly city, wrote St Augustine of Hippo, forms around the common objects, not subjects, of love. Community, in other words, is grounded in concerns beyond ourselves. The unfolding climate emergency – the Anthropocene's greatest test – asks questions of our love (for God, land, neighbour) and demands that we return to the ground. This is something of a shock for those who grew up believing that the global village would enable us to transcend local allegiance. In fact, fairly emphatically, it has indicated the opposite.

A generation ago, the sociologist Anthony Giddens contended that the 'disembedding' of social relations was a distinctive feature of late or 'high' modernity, as he labelled the present age. Indeed, the modern era could be defined by this progressive detachment of experience from time, space and tradition, as global relations became ever more extended, especially with the advance of electronic communications. For Giddens and other social theorists of this period, such a process was the inevitable outworking of capitalism, always inimical to local or societal constraints. The market aspires to transcendence, and has long sought to be boundless.

Yet despite modernity's remarkable conquest of space–time – market-driven or not – human culture inevitably falls to earth. Global shifts, whether in commerce, conflict or climate, are always a local matter. Moreover, it is clear that our hubristic detachment from place has the ironical consequence of fuelling demand for at least the appearance of locality and authenticity (witness the proliferation of micro-level businesses, 'craft' produce and so on). Society is reckoning with nostalgia – literally the 'longing for home' – on a global scale, and because neoliberals are unsuited to dealing sympathetically with the political fallout, populist movements have stepped forward to claim the territory.

The Brexit referendum – so injurious to our political tradition and, by consequence, national unity – has sharpened society's edges and continues to saw away at the ties binding the United Kingdom. Devolution, however, leaves the English feeling somewhat undressed: ashamed at our nakedness, conscious of our gross failings and unfitness. Britain (in a European coat, perhaps) has been our national clothing – the form in which we feel able to see and consider ourselves. We don't talk about England in the same way we don't talk about God, maybe because the two have been so intimately associated. Unable easily to address either without embarrassment, the country must find a new kind of liturgy, of both penitence and thanksgiving: a common prayer.

English Grounds grew from a conviction that the Church I served had a foundational stake in this nation's story, for better and worse – and a desire that (especially when experiencing a crisis of collective identity) we should attend far more than formerly to what 'of England' might now mean. It felt to me as if this affiliation was forever in parentheses – as though it were a love that dare not speak its name. I had a fairly good idea why, but thought that if we could recover confidence in that qualifying description, it could be a gift to benefit everyone, regardless of denomination.

In my previous book *Parish*, I had begun to explore the

idea that a nation (or a world, for that matter) is what you end up – not begin – with. This appeared to be the rationale not only of physics and organic growth, but also of Christian theology. In Jesus Christ, it is believed, God takes place. That means Christians tend to answer universal questions in a very particular way – starting at Nazareth and working outwards, inferring cosmic truths from local ones. The culture of the kingdom, Jesus taught, springs from something small – yeast, say, or a seed – with potential for unlimited increase.

The more I delved, the more 'parish' seemed to be a fractal of 'England', and I became convinced that renewing the former was a clue to redeeming the whole. The principal difficulty in the prevailing political climate was that both words were locked into an outdated caricature that could not help but appear monocultural and reactionary. Parish is a bond-word: a covenant with place. Deeply rooted within Western culture, it expresses our need for a footing in the world, for local attachment. Consequently, the parish idea is not only highly potent – binding secular to sacred, human community to natural landscape – but also problematic and politicized, encapsulating the tensions contained in our desire to belong. Evoking an idyll of (typically rural) settlement, the extended form 'parochial' is mostly employed in the derogatory sense of blinkered insularity: the social drawbridge slammed shut. For those watching in dismay at the growth of national movements across Europe, the new parochialism was a doubly bad thing, denoting both fear of the outsider and the retrogressive urge to regain an Edenic past.

That the word 'parish' has such a painful dual edge is down to its unusual blend of associations. In ancient Graeco-Roman society its original form *paroikia* described the community of people either living physically beyond city boundaries (literally, 'those beside the house') or as non-citizens within the walls – those who lived nearby, but didn't quite belong. It is painfully ironic that 'parochial' came to epitomize petty-minded self-containment, when its original meaning indicates the opposite and is far closer to our contemporary definitions of 'stranger' or 'refugee'. The effective transition in meaning, from 'outsider' to 'insider', came about when the early Church adopted 'parish' as a description of its own local form. The Christian *paroikia* were those who didn't belong in a worldly sense, yet had found a new kind of ideal home, a heavenly destination.

Today, we urgently require models of society that can be resilient without being defensive – 'little' without being narrow – as the building blocks of a post-Covid settlement. In rural and urban communities alike (and the suburban shades between them, where most of us live), chronic alienation is the curse of our times. Place-formation at any level grows from shared stories in a shared landscape, so it is a grievous mistake to think that this is somehow the fixed possession of one class or ethnic group. National identity has often been associated with race and ethnicity because these have been assumed to represent unity and tradition, both of which are key components of cultural belonging. But if nations are (as the historian Benedict Anderson contended) 'imagined communities', existing as much in the mind as on the ground, it should not require much imagination to rethink, for example, the myopic view that 'Englishness' is an intrinsically racial – expressly 'white' – descriptor.

Debates about national character are a vain pursuit, but the simple point is that this evolves, along with our language and culture. 'English', being a more affective word than the plainly generic 'British', is something you either feel or you don't – so the challenge for all, like me, who do (especially when we acquire power and privilege) is to address the reasons why so many do not. We might begin by confessing the error often made by those who find they belong – which is to suppose that places, as a consequence, belong to them.

Myths of possessing the land can only collapse unless it is seen as both ours and not ours. Above all – in Scripture, at least – the earth is the Lord's. This is why love of home can turn stagnant unless refreshed by outward-facing love of neighbour – that basic moral posture in which we are ready and willing to give up our seat for others. As in the railway carriage, so in the cosmos: 'Let there be ...' is the logic of creation. Growing national identity from a commitment to neighbourhood does not spare us the squabbling obsessions of place, as anyone involved in local politics knows. But it may foster a narrative where common good meets common ground, and which values short stories as preciously as the long, multi-season saga.

I am writing this introduction at the start of Lent: an old English word binding Christian spirituality to seasonal time and the fields beneath us. The country is also still in the wilderness of Lockdown, when so many have redis-covered – indeed, come to depend upon – the gift of local ecology. I am conscious of what a blessing it is to have been transplanted into this ancient, mystical landscape for such a time of confinement, and what began as an idea for a collection of essays soon became a personal journal of an exceptional period in which this new home county has been both revelation and lasting gift. Somewhat acci-dentally, it also emerged as a celebration of the ongoing significance of church buildings, and those who heroically sustain them.

This book is, then, partly a hymn from Wiltshire: one newcomer's reckoning with a parcel of soil that has inspired so much lyricism. In his novel *The Longest Journey*, E. M. Forster wrote that 'The fibres of England unite in Wiltshire.'[1] Hyperbole, of course – and every corner of the country could eloquently tell an authentic national tale. But there are particular traces in this gate-way to the South West that illustrate a narrative vital to understand in order to write the future. The collection here is entirely occasional, being field notes from the places I happen to have encountered over the last two years. They offer, therefore, a very partial, rural and autobiographical set of sketches that makes no bid at being comprehensive. The pieces are arranged chronologically: beginning and ending in the bleak weeks of Epiphany, just ahead of the Lenten wilderness.

The long route out from the pandemic's shadowy vale will require some bold and imaginative mapping, not least from what remains – even nominally – the national Church. In searching for a new English settlement, our contribution may yet prove fruitful, being foolish enough to believe that we are bound for a better place.

Ash Wednesday 2021

Far from the halogen gleam

Nature doesn't dwell on the past. Last Sunday's snowfall – a joyous overnight arrival, pulling a wintry balaclava over the village – had given ground by evening, with each white-mittened branch brittle and brown again. Along the River Kennet, its thaw has saturated the water meadows behind our garden. Attempting to walk across this morning I find a new river has appeared, eeling through the field as if it had always been there.

The emergence of a stream is a holy thing, welling unbidden from hidden altars. And it strikes me that the axis of the spirit generally tends towards *y* not *x*: *de profundis* is the soul's cry and, for some, this becomes the borehole of eternal life. 'In the obscure recesses of our being (the mystic will assert), we near the gates of the divine' wrote E. M. Forster, sounding the creative impulse. 'As it came from the depths, so it soars to the heights, out of local questionings.' This intersection – where the psyche breaks the surface – can be a place of crisis and also renewal, having an artesian effect that spills into our environment.

I was first drawn by underground water when living in south-east London twenty years ago. As Vicar of Gipsy Hill (a small parish near Crystal Palace Park, with an unparalleled vista of the capital), I found that the Effra – a tributary of the River Thames and a Celtic word meaning 'torrent' – rose just yards from my church. Though culverted into the sewer system by practical Victorians, it reappeared periodically: neighbours would show where the grass grew greener and their flowers bloomed more vividly in back gardens where it passed beneath. I even met an elderly man who had been fished out of the Effra as an infant: when in spate it swamped the West Norwood streets soon after World War One. He owed his life to the local butcher who had plunged in after him.

I became quite consumed with pursuing my local lost river, hearing in the course of parish life all manner of stories that dowsed this fascination. Being concealed under a concrete coat only added to the mystique, increased the longing to go deeper. Road names – Brixton Water Lane, Effra Road – offered clues to its invisible path, which I would pace and plot, straining eccentrically with my ear to drainage covers at which you could listen to it surge; dodging security cameras by the MI6 building in Vauxhall where it emerges into the Thames. I formed a band that borrowed its name, wrote songs about the river's route and performed them at the closest pubs we could find, in a meandering kind of pilgrimage. One of our haunts, the Half Moon in Herne Hill, was closed for four years after floods overwhelmed the vicinity in 2013.

Standing by the Kennet, it is consoling for me to be linked with South London by a single veining network of water, draining into the Thames. And this is worth recalling because the well-beaten boundary between country and city is often presented as a battlefield of urban encroachment. Variegated campaigns in the last century show how easy it is for those defending the countryside to set the built environment in antithesis: an imagined separation that idealizes or mummifies the rural and downplays the proximity of nature to urban landscapes. Ignoring this interdependence has also left ruralists prone to illegitimate myths of Englishness that are likewise presented as 'under threat'.

Yet if we seek depth, whatever our situation, the sense of personal space expands, even – and perhaps especially – in confinement. Place-making is, in this sense, cruciform, and requires looking down before we look out. It concerns the relation between portrait and landscape: also, if we hear it, the call to leave our earthly Edens for a visionary city, through which (it is written) runs the crystalline river of life.

The grey wethers

Epiphany weighs the gift, asks us: 'What will you do with what has been given?' Sifting the stockinged ephemera from things of lasting value.

This morning I am out early on Overton Hill, where begins Britain's oldest road, the Ridgeway: a Neolithic trade route that extends some eighty-seven miles to Ivinghoe Beacon in the Chilterns. I am looking for the sarsen fields on Fyfield Down, a uniquely abundant scattering of these remnants of the post-glacial landscape. The local Lego from which the mystic architecture of Avebury and Stonehenge was artfully fixed and propped, these sandstone nuggets may have been deposited as meltwater washed and rushed into the Kennet valley, panning the silt that hitherto embedded them.

Thus sieved out and served on to the surface, sarsen (either Wiltshire dialect for 'saracen' – that is, strangers from the East – or 'sar-sten' in Anglo-Saxon, meaning 'troublesome stone') is one of this landscape's oddest offerings. They are also known as Grey Wethers, having from afar the appearance of sheep. On approach, my myopia certainly bore this out: a hundred yards off, I was still unsure whether or not this distant congregation was rock or flock – until one of them moved. A whisper of disappointment, followed by hilarity at thinking that creatures so shocked with the divine electricity of life could be less impressive than something stock still and insentient.

Sarsens are the same size as sheep and, on Fyfield Down, graze the same spot, so that one looks like the transfixed form of the other, caught in a game of statues. Striding through their playground, monitor eyes turned and gazed my way, so that, for a few seconds, I found myself entirely beheld. Fyfield Down has been worked for some 7,000 years, its scrabble of tracks, mounds and ridges left for us to read and arrange as we will. This is tradition: to reinterpret the encrypted past, while the turn is ours.

For many centuries, the awkward boulders hereabouts – even those in sacred arrangements – were heaved out of the way where they impeded the future. While much was lost and vandalized (even Victorian visitors to Stonehenge could hire small hammers to hack off a souvenir), our fenced-off reverence for heritage feels petrified by comparison – as if time is up. The present is an animated interval in which we live and move and have our being. Knowing this doesn't last and that soon we shall sleep, while stones become sheep for others, is a spur to motion – a memory of myrrh.

All along the Wansdyke

A spaniel pauses, front paw cocked and poised: on the verge of something. Dogless yet (despite crumbling defences), I'm in the minority on these hills, where every rambler has their hound.

'The boundary lines have fallen for me in pleasant places', sang the Psalmist, a verse that suits finding the Wansdyke: a striking sub-Roman earthwork that spreads in two wings, east and west, between Bath and Marlborough. The most well-preserved stretches are here, along the soft shoulders of the Pewsey Vale, near the long barrow known as Adam's Grave. In the year 592, according to the Anglo-Saxon Chronicle, 'there was great slaughter in Britain' on this site, in a clash between the Anglo-Saxons in Wessex and the British tribes in Mercia, northwards. Plausibly, this was because of a crossing point in the Wansdyke nearby, funnelling rival armies on to the hillside, into a mash of blood and woad.

A large, lone stone, about half a mile from Adam's Grave, is – a fellow-walker assures me – not one of the sarsens scattered like dice hereabouts, but a distance marker for marching armies traversing the Wansdyke. I had viewed this chap ahead, orange Gore-tex moving like a laser pinpoint along the path, and caught up with him above the mane of the Alton Barnes white horse, where he now stood, its miniature jockey. Breezing along together, he told me how, every so often, he will come and camp out on this hill, simply because of its glorious solitude. Back home, I imagined him as a grizzled St Peter, returning to his mount of transfiguration. It was good to be here, we agreed.

At length, we reached the Wansdyke – sometimes known as the Devil's or Ealden (ancient) dyke, but now settled, like Wednesday, as a Chinese whisper of the Germanic god Woden. While Bede's *Ecclesiastical History* lists him as the great-grandfather of Anglo-Saxon *arrivistes* Hengist and Horsa, Woden – perhaps more than King Arthur – was a legendary figure for the early English. Among other attributes, he was a god of boundaries, which would explain the ditch's earliest ascription: *Woden's dic*. No one is entirely clear why or when such an imposing trench – still pretty deep – was placed here, although opinion now favours an origin in the fifth century, possibly as a division of Roman *civitates* against the threatening Dobunni tribe, to the north. That a later battle between Wessex and

Mercia was chronicled on this site, in 715, bears witness to the continuing, unfathomable power of drawing a line.

What force, divine or not, makes us score the ground so, like cuts on a butcher's chart? The need to defend and define our pitch lies deep as Adam's grave, such that the crossing of boundaries has always been an action both sacred and dangerous. Maybe we have come too far East of Eden, but a gap in the Wansdyke today reveals no flaming, switching sword: just a silver Ford, parked on a private road. The course of the ditch curves away like a spine; running back down its length sends up a shiver of birds.

The consolation of England

Candlemas, and the land awaits its consolation, Simeon-like. Unfurling woes roll out so regularly that media feeds read like Qoheleth, a psalmody of untethered lament. The temptation is to withdraw into immediacy, of course, and purely field the incoming as if sat in a gaming chair of perpetual reaction, spotting and batting away the next insurgent.

When we cry for strategy perhaps what we really mean is prophecy – strategy being inorganic, mechanistic, hardly adequate for the times. After all, how do you map a scene that is constantly changing? Our present panic seeks good words from the world to come, where no one but God has been. But in an age that sniggers away divine possibility the Lord is afforded the past tense alone. We shall, I suspect, come to regret being so confident of our own purposelessness. Behold, mourns the weary preacher of the book of Ecclesiastes, all is vanity and vexation of spirit.

What characterizes his world is a kind of dogged amnesia: collapsing past and future into a monotonous present. 'There is no remembrance of former things; neither shall there be any remembrance of things that are to come with those that shall come after.' Like the rivers, he suggests, that run into the sea before their ascension and condensation start the cycle again. But what if repetition is not our destiny, and we inhabit instead an ecology that is radically open? What if our absent-minded land were a place of promise, and we had simply forgotten?

Prophecy returns to the origins of things in order to seek and sketch what is to come. So, after its overflow last week, I am drawn to revisit Swallowhead Spring, near

Avebury in Wiltshire, where the River Kennet rises and begins to drain down into the Thames. Like many such sites round here, the signage indicates conflicting claims on this landscape. A 'Pagan Britain' sticker has been slapped upon an anti-littering notice and the trees are frilly with ribbons and dangling dream catchers, the symbolism of which escapes me. What is clear, however, is the enduring need to mark territories where meaning or identity has been found: our arrow-hearted initials notched into the bark. Lovers and villagers would apparently come to Swallowhead Spring for Good Friday picnics, before shinning up the then-accessible Silbury Hill. When I last visited in October, it was just a dry basin with a slightly sludgy brook, but now I can hardly approach for the cataract.

Back home, a bubble-wrapped book has arrived, being the proceedings of the 1941 Malvern Conference: a source I am exploring for clues to the current and future condition of the beleaguered English Church. Under the shroud of total war, Archbishop William Temple gathered an eclectic range of prelates, poets and politicians to devise a route by which the Church might offer a lead to society in the new world that would, at some point, emerge. It is immediately striking in its erudition and reach, addressing the fundamental concern that 'the true end of man' had lately been obscured by the pursuit of wealth.

The purpose of work and education, therefore, needed recovering – but with personality, not product, at its heart. Progress was, however, almost derailed by a Christian Socialist attack on private property, which T. S. Eliot, among other conservative delegates, rebuffed. Hard, perhaps, to imagine the same debate stirring such feeling today, although any consideration of social justice surely must. As H. G. Wells once observed, from the earliest times society was a mitigation of ownership – the mutual recognition that co-operation needed to override competitive possession if humanity was to flourish. The matter was finessed at Malvern in fine Anglican style, with the following resolution:

> It is a traditional doctrine of Christendom that property is necessary to fulness of personal life; all citizens should be enabled to hold such property as contributes to moral independence and spiritual freedom without impairing that of others; but where the rights of property conflict with the establishment of social justice or the general social welfare, those rights should be overridden, modified, or, if need be, abolished.[2]

This was synthesis, not fudge, I choose to think – and helpful in reaching a similar conclusion lately, while trying to locate my true north, politically speaking. The conservative in me tends towards continuity, local institutions and the Parable of the Talents, in its acknowledgement of unequal gift and yield; the radical abhors squandered privilege and exploitation of the poor for personal gain. Naboth's vineyard may be the place, therefore, given that I am firmly in favour of covenantal ownership, which either serves the common good or is reckoned to be in deficit.

The conservative fallacy is to recycle the sins and sinecures of our forebears and call it tradition; the equivalent on the Left is to be perpetually uprooting and call it liberty. Amid their own peculiar failings, the Christian has – somehow – both to belong and not belong, to possess all and yet nothing, in search of a country that is forever ahead.

Without a city wall

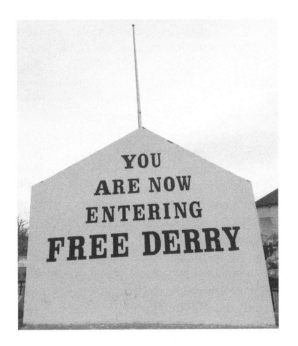

A frayed hole in the shoulder of a boy's coat. His photograph, moments before the puncturing bullet. Plum-coloured stains on that day's clothes, pegged up, unwashed. Remembrance is forensic here.

The Museum of Free Derry, site of the Bloody Sunday shootings in January 1972, is a perpetual crime scene: an open wound of wailing tarmac. Every rag and relic, each faded veronica, devotedly kept on display. And what pains the aggrieved have taken, that we might stay to see what they still see. Images superimposed on a window overlooking the car park mark the precise place where our guide's brother fell, or where desperate friends carried another's slumping frame. An insistent haunting, this.

Traumatic memory is prone to being replayed, scarring places and people like a scratch in a record. Events as explosive, as jarring as these, are a barricade to the normal processions of time and space, and none of us is equipped to move beyond them. A cycle of violence is just that: a hurt we return to. Revolutions are rarely progressive, merely re-enactment.

Perhaps this begins to explain why, in Londonderry – the only complete walled city in Ireland – the past remains so encompassing, and so well preserved. Bloodshed seizes our attention, naturally enough, but more compelling yet are Derry's deep continuities and astounding powers of recall. The siege of the city in 1689 by the Catholic king James II – recently deposed from the English throne and looking to Ireland to regather his powers – moulded and cast the cultural imagination here. To keep this intact, the Apprentice Boys of Derry Association, named after thirteen youths who slammed the Derry doors against Jacobite forces (and whose relentless marching pounds their rebuttal into the landscape), has its own, intensely curated, museum. Within these walls there is no surrender to time, and history without relief.

Such a concentrated defence of territory and tradition, spiked as it is with the bayonet of religious difference, feels uneasily biblical. On hallowed ground local actions – British Army emplacements along the walls during the Troubles, for example – become inescapably prophetic and provocative: all things become soaked in their associations. Including (it sinks in pretty swiftly) ourselves: Anglican visitors, implicated up to our collars in our nation's anaesthetic detachment from the fallout of her history. For, *pace* John Lydon, there is no past in England's dreaming: its sparks no longer ignite us. We can incinerate Guy Fawkes without a singe to our skin.

But upon these clouded hills, Derry (the 'London' prefix being an English branding) feels like a British Jerusalem. So there is an aptness to the fact that Cecil Frances Alexander, who married the Anglican Bishop of Derry, wrote her enduring Good Friday hymn, 'There is a Green Hill Far Away', gazing on the prospect from these battlements, where our clutch of clergy musters for its tour. How do we deal with crucifying memories, beyond amnesia or fretful repetition? This is a question our guides – two priests, one Catholic and one Protestant – are committed to answering together, to finding within their sufferings the secrets of agreement. Peace is, in their view, a new anamnesis.

On Bogside, a stone's throw below, the former scrawl of the Free Derry Corner has become more pristine, more carefully typographical, with each successive repainting. Insurgency turned into heritage, a national mistrust. The bus was quiet returning to Belfast: our pilgrim's tread now soft, like trespass.

Dieu et mon droit

Rivers silver the fields, and every forded lane conceals a range of jarring potholes. This grim and unrelenting rain seems to have been with us since September: buffeted by Sunday's alphabetical storm, I'm beginning to think a barge would have been a better bet than my low-lying Volvo.

Completing the slalom, I turn up at Great Durnford for their ten-thirty service. Even by this county's standards, St Andrew's Church is exceptionally well preserved for fittings and furniture. One could call it a time capsule, except that each item (Cromwellian pulpit, sciatica-inflaming fourteenth-century pews and 900-year-old font) is being used for its original purpose, so there is an unbroken chain of memory and practice. Whatever else they are, village churches are not museums. And on the north wall, an unfaded royal coat of arms dated 1678, bearing the legend 'Feare God, honour the king' and listing the churchwardens of that year (including one John Pile, whose surname reappears on the roll of honour for World War One).

These boards are a common feature of older parish churches. Often so age-darkened as to display only an outline of lion or smudge of unicorn, they remain as an emblem of the compact between Church and state. Some were installed, as embroidered hangings, after Henry VIII's break with Rome: many more after the Restoration of the monarchy in 1660, badging an era when, as Linda Colley puts it in her fine book *Britons*, 'Protestantism was the foundation that made the invention of Great Britain possible.'[3]

The curse of British Christianity (also, at times, its blessing) is that it has proved so politically useful. Surprisingly, enduringly so – from its early expression as the integrating principle behind the merger of the Anglo-Saxon kingdoms, through the vagaries of the English Revolution, to providing the moral underpinnings of the Welfare State in the 1930s and 1940s – still the clearest articulation of (albeit secularized) homegrown Christian socialism.

It is hard to avoid the fact that, at each step-change, the Church not only provided divine sanction for monarchic interest, but (more significantly, I think) also gave narrative meaning to national destiny. As 'Britishness' emerged into a coherent concept in the eighteenth century ('Rule Britannia', for example, was composed in 1740, with the national anthem appearing five years later, sung in a London theatre, to ecstatic encores), the Church of England reinforced the new social contract like a hessian-backed map.

Perhaps Edmund Burke was right in reflecting that we would avert revolution on the French scale through the strength of this association at the local level – so bluntly hammered into the wall here at Great Durnford. Yet the cost of this conscription into the national cause has been severe – allying military success with the will of God, justifying the crimes of empire and slavery, and a deep investment in commercial profit and landed wealth. More radical visions of the Christian nation have tended to emerge (from, say, Milton, Maurice or Temple) only when the Church re-engaged with the narrative arc of Scripture, rather than all-too-plastic notions of 'providence' that appear to bless us without qualification. Eschatology may sound unhinged, but is our exit from nationalism.

'A nation', wrote Ernest Renan, 'is a soul, a spiritual principle.' It is also, he added, 'an everyday plebiscite'[4] that requires the ongoing assent of its people to a common idea. Under those terms, Christian heritage – as a lifeless deposit – is of limited value. Living tradition, however, has political currency. We have little idea of Britain at present – and enough of plebiscites to last us a lifetime. If the Church is to inform a new national polity, it must decide again how to be useful – and at what price.

Unfathomable mines

Shrove Tuesday by the sliced tomb of Richard III. We have just evensung William Cowper's irresistible line from 'God Moves in a Mysterious Way', about the Almighty working out his purpose 'deep in unfathomable mines', as though his *logos* were a pick. If divine will was being hacked out in the fantastic journey of Richard Plantagenet's bones through Bosworth Field and municipal tarmac, it was from a low and peculiar shaft. The monarch's mausoleum is nonetheless an oddly holy and transfixing spot: like his incredible recovery, it feels felicitous.

The civic church of St Martin was hallowed as Leicester Cathedral in 1927, halfway through my grandfather's long tenure as Rector of Quorn, a country parish ten miles from here. Marbled albums and stuffed, buff envelopes have passed down the pastoralia, but behind these clipped-out Anglican ghosts, in eight volumes of incomprehension, lie Henry Rumsey's diaries. We have all tried to read it, this tight and indecipherable hand, and while parts are plain – service times, small sums owed, or an underlined text ('what I do thou knowest not now, but thou shalt know hereafter') – most is opaque. The one break in writing – six months from September 1921, when his beloved wife Lilian died, leaving my four-month-old father and five further children – is really the clearest thing.

Cheese straws and celery sticks after the service. Lent's little apocalypse happens to land this year on the anniversary of Dad's death, making this a wake of sorts, filed around Richard's snaking spine. Ash Wednesday brings its relief of renunciation: a reassurance that mortal things can and ought to stop – and that the nature of their end endows our lives with meaning. God's Will works in reverse: Lent is old earth flung from death's graveside, as if to say 'the time of dying is bound to die'. Each soiled forehead, like a bud, is a bid on life, and daftly prophetic.

Afterwards, digging into the family archive, I find cuttings from the *Leicester Mercury* that report the 'imposing pageant' of the cathedral's establishment – joyously, on the Sunday before Lent 1927. 'In hallowing Leicester, the city and the county', preached the Bishop of Winchester, 'you are hallowing anew just those qualities of our English Christianity that we need to re-establish in our land today. For our industrial civilization needs to be continually corrected and purified by the things of the spirit.' He cites seven saints of Leicestershire, culminating with Archbishop William Laud: 'his methods were mistaken. His ideals were magnificent. A well-ordered state; a deep conviction of the dignity of public life; a passionate hatred of all that is petty, sectional and factious and a fearless application of Christian principles to private life. They were never more needed than now.'

Over in Quorn, Henry was taking up his pen: 'I am the Lord which halloweth you', I can read. The rest is unclear.

At Semington Base

Lemon and lime grit bins, vivid against a drab driveway. Arriving at the headquarters of Wiltshire Air Ambulance, the same scheme adorns the Bell 429 now alighting on the helipad: flattening the field with its deafening blast. Helicopters are lethal miracles: something to do with all that vast force being employed to keep the thing suspended in one place. Setting torque against torque, they're a strangely effective kind of civil war: flailing, yet contained – like The Kinks. Feuding guitarists in a teenage bedroom; jar-bound wasps, watched through glass.

This is a tour for faith leaders of the charity's luminous new base, hived away near the village of Semington. Our interested circle hovers through reception, past promotional teddies and breakout space, upstairs to where an extraordinary fundraising dynamo generates the £10,000 needed each day to stay aloft. With operations constantly fanning past the window, the work offered up has an immediacy that mobilizes everyone.

In the operations room, we see Wiltshire mapped by emergency, and the wit, skill and resilience of the paramedics, whose team attends, on average, three potentially lifesaving missions each day. Anywhere in the county can be reached within eleven minutes, they say, as an alert sends the crew out again. Every flight like a Johannine angel: ascending and descending upon the Son of Man.

Away from the escalating din, an interactive simulation room reveals the hazards attending their arrival at an incident. Last summer, the Air Ambulance was grounded for tests, amid fears of contamination by Novichok, though everyday things can also become terrible in an instant. A sandpit, tarpaulin or half-opened window: all would be whisked up and into the blades by two tonnes of recirculated air. The pilots, many ex-military, say it is the reactive nature of the flying they enjoy, but it must be like landing a whirlwind.

Apparently, the helipad sits on the precise site of a Romano-British shrine – one of only four in the country – and on the way back, via Devizes, I call in at some of its Christian successors, each one a pledge on transcendence. In the porch of St George's, Semington, I find a thirteenth-century inscription in Norman French. The translation reads: 'Whoever shall say a Pater Noster and an Ave-Maria for the souls, for Philippa de Salcest, and Christians, shall have 40 days of pardon'. An odd contract to bid for, and long expired. Then, in the lofty atmospherics of Seend Church, a small stone Madonna, defaced in some brutal occurrence. Her ruffled sleeves, still vaguely blue, cradle an infant Christ: present at the scene.

Virginia Ash

Two pieces of badger, so evenly pared and laid that my car passes between them like Abram's smoking fire pot. This quick covenant made with the land, I descend through Wiltshire and down into Dorset for Sunday worship at Sherborne Abbey. And along the A30, the Virginia Ash inn, recalling the ignition of Sir Walter Raleigh's pipe on this spot – thus provoking his servant's famed sprinkler system. There is a 'Raleigh Room' (to be fair, an outside shelter) at the pub where his burnt offering may be re-enacted. Tobacco remained so central to Raleigh's myth that he mentions it – as the means of effecting his return home – in a last letter to his wife, from his final, fatal expedition to find El Dorado in 1618.

Raleigh, who appropriated Sherborne Castle from the Bishop of Salisbury and worshipped at the abbey, came from a crop of Elizabethans who (as the late Richard Helgerson writes, in his brilliant book *Forms of Nationhood*) undertook 'a concerted generational project ... the writing of England'.[5] Whether by verse, overseas voyages or the new discipline of 'chorography' – the systematic mapping of the land – the focus of this unfurling interest was the country itself, and the definition of its place in the world. The impetus was the split from Rome of the English Church and the subsequent need, as Raleigh puts it in his *History of the World*, to 'set together the unjointed and scattered frame of our English affairs'.[6]

Navigating the place of England (Britain being, for now, out of focus) was a route charted chiefly by Christian theology. Helgerson sees two distinct schools emerging during Elizabeth's reign – the apocalyptic and the apologetic – the tension between which would eventually wrench the nation apart at the Civil War. The former, typified by Foxe's grisly martyrology *Acts and Monuments*, fuelled sectarian dissent and puzzled out an equation between the end times as depicted by the book of Revelation and the present state of the nation. The latter – of which Richard Hooker's *Of the Laws of Ecclesiastical Polity* remains the acme – sought not to set God's elect apart, or afloat on some Mayflowering mission, but argued instead for settled conformity to a national Church. The twin halves of *Leviathan*, Thomas Hobbes's foundational treatise on political science, illustrate how, half a century later, English polity remained (in Helgerson's words) 'cut up the middle'.

After a croissant with the chaplain we are into Sherborne Abbey, where I am preaching to a thousand teenagers at their school service. The temptation of Christ is the theme, this being the First in Lent, and I hope to speak about the danger of making life decisions based solely on what the multitude might affirm, even if that separates you out, somehow. This, and my youthful 'experiments with an amen', praying in bathrooms at parties.

Founded in AD 705, the abode of at least two kings of Wessex; seat of Asser, King Alfred's scribe and of John Jewel – next to Hooker, the greatest of the Anglican apologists – the abbey, as you enter, astonishes. All you can do is look up, for it seems like the ceiling of heaven. Fan vaulting fountains out in delicate webs, with every pillar a slim Elizabethan neck, decked and ruffed for the courts of praise. Here below, between piles of stacking chairs, reclines a bisected priest in charred stone. His prone prayers have left him in pieces: neatly, but completely cracked.

A clink in the locks

Descending into Potterne from Devizes you veer through the village, steered by an antique road sign, gemmed with reflector studs. In Wiltshire, the years do not readily give way. Among other treasures, this former manor of the bishops of Salisbury retains along its high street an extraordinary survivor from the fifteenth-century-named Porch House: timber bones now crutched with scaffold, mere inches from the rumbling Scanias along the A360.

I am driving to see another experiment in time and space, Erlestoke Prison. Situated along the north-western rim of Salisbury Plain, within earshot of the guns' low thump, HMP Erlestoke is a Category C men's prison, with a vacant chaplain's post for the high proportion of inmates who identify as Anglican. The day is brisk and blue and, beside the looming perimeter, an honesty stall sells eggs and primroses.

Prison visits, with their perpetually supervised movement and routines of locking and unlocking, are intense lessons in human geography. In his influential work *Discipline and Punish*, Michel Foucault asserted that prisons (along with schools, factories and garrisons) epitomize the 'panoptic' institutions of modernity, where strict surveillance is the clue to power.[7] At Erlestoke, it is not so much observation as controlled access to space that is most affecting. Marshalling men back into their cells in order that vulnerable prisoners may pass or fraternize is a constant source of tension: possession of social space – even temporary – is acutely felt and highly charged. Quite remarkable what wire, walls and doors do to the human psyche: compressing it to the point of combustion.

In such a force field, the chapel holds peculiar attraction for, despite being hemmed by the same boundaries, it is simply – the chaplain avers – 'a different kind of space'. If the prison is one sort of 'heterotopia' (a term Michel Foucault employed in his influential 1967 essay 'Of Other Spaces: Utopias and Heterotopias'),[8] then the prison chapel is, palpably, another still. Heterotopias are described as places where time and space are extracted from their normal passage and heightened or preserved, as in a museum, or theatre. Holy space is in this sense a deliberate construct – a circumscription that sets aside a portion of ordinary ground and declares that, within these bounds, we shall live as though heaven's door were ajar.

Being a glimpse of eternity (which, my doctrine tutor would insist, we must imagine as *'more and more*, not on and on' – as it were an expansion, not just an extended sentence), the prison chapel indicates freedom not from, but *within* confinement – the content, I recall, of St Paul's biblical plea to Philemon. From his own incarceration, Paul, 'a prisoner of Christ Jesus', commends to his friend's care the returning slave Onesimus, whose newfound faith brings liberation, even amid bondage. What the key of David opens, no one will shut.

Copies of *Inside Time*, the prisoners' and detainees' newspaper, litter the restroom at Erlestoke as I leave, relieved. Whether we strive to conquer time or find ourselves captive to it, each of us is, in W. H. Auden's words, 'in the cell of themselves'.[9] A clink in the locks, one sharp turn and I'm away.

Pelican in the wilderness

'We have a dehumanization suit', advises my companion. This is David Waters, executive officer for the Great Bustard Group, a pioneering Wiltshire charity that has doggedly succeeded in reintroducing the world's heaviest flying bird to Salisbury Plain, nearly 200 years after the last poor specimen was shot and stuffed. The suit, he explains, here in the Group's compound near the village of Enford, is donned in order to feed and rear the chicks without being identifiably human – achieved in part by its colour scheme. Neither his Land Rover, nor hammering gunfire from the Challenger tanks of the King's Royal Hussars, alarms the birds, as would a watchful human form – and you can understand them being a little wary.

Mayors of Salisbury traditionally feasted on roast bustard, the county's emblem, which now struts at the centre of the Wiltshire flag, against green and white arcs of chalk downland. It is also engraved on the cover of *Birds of Wiltshire* from 1887, by parson-naturalist, antiquarian and sometime Vicar of Yatesbury, the Reverend A. C. Smith. Despite the bird having then been extinct for over half a century, Smith nevertheless devotes to it some twenty-six pages. Boyhood outrage about the dodo was, for David Waters, the spring from which his own interest arose – quickened on finding a British equivalent on his doorstep. While the great bustard is about the same height (the male standing at about three feet), its huge, angelic, eight-foot wingspan is incomparable. Waters's campaign, involving ten dogged years in the Russian countryside sourcing eggs, began in 2004 and his patient tenacity has resulted in there being today about a hundred bustards on the Plain, with more added each year on 'soft release' – the avian equivalent, he explains, of allowing your teenagers gradually to stray from home until they leave.

Inevitably, some are snatched by foxes (although, pleasingly, they can outrun Reynard, at speeds of up to 30 m.p.h.) and others fly away – one went to the Loire Valley, yet homed again to Wiltshire, another to Toulouse, where they remain, *en vacances*. But within minutes of turning on to the prohibited central ranges, we are able to locate a 'drove' of about thirty great bustards, noticeable in a rape field half a mile away by a semaphore of white flashes, as the male bustards' springtime mating displays begin. Apart from their airborne reputation, they are also known for extreme sexual dimorphism – such that the males can grow to four to five times the size of the female. Viewed through a telescope this contrast is clear, as the rear of one behemoth erupts into a milky froth of tail feathers.

'I am become like a pelican in the wilderness', writes the Psalmist, in the Book of Common Prayer. 'I have watched, and am even as it were a sparrow that sitteth alone upon the house-top.' The remoteness of birds as a motif for our own seclusion is worth pondering in this uncertain season – as, too, is their mysterious resilience.

Hagioscope

In alabaster, with his hound, Sir Roger Tocotes lies. His tomb, from 1492, emphatically life-sized, is a visitor's book of crooked graffiti. Roundhead troops, Sunday school pupils, even two former rectors have initialled every inch of him, until he has two coats indeed – one the clean, cream surface and another this riot of tattoos, an insistent *Who's Who*.

There is no service being held at St Nicholas, Bromham, but rarely have I stood in a church so crowded with absentees. At every turn a Dives, needing to be heard from eternity. 'As I was, so are yee: as I am, so shall you bee', implores an inscription on the north wall, with a winding sheet, skull and crossed thigh bones (the minimum a soul would require for resurrection, it was supposed) under a pregnant hourglass. *Settle down, everyone*, I want to say.

Stillness in solitude, even in an ancient church, isn't always easy to achieve. Whether or not the walls around us are as busily tracked as these, each place pesters for our attention. And we, too, are a palimpsest of sorts: overwritten by all that presses in upon us. As soon as we try to calm ourselves – for prayer or just a moment apart – a demonstration begins, diverting us with placarding thoughts. The only way I know to field this protest is to usher it up and away as worship.

Contemplatives have, accordingly, tended to simplify their surroundings, often to an extreme degree. As an anchorite, Mother Julian of Norwich was bricked into a small and doorless space attached to a church, her brilliant visions assisted by three tiny windows: one for light, one to pass in food, and another through which to view the

Eucharist. Love for Christ made one little room an every-where.

The third of these openings, known as *hagioscopes*, were a means of squinting upon the holy mysteries for those who, through sickness, status or sanctity, had to observe social distancing. There is one here in Bromham Church, hacked through the tower pillar. Given ill-health and holiness both involve being set apart, how do we view communion in a time of quarantine? In 1559, John Calvin, addressing our connection to an exalted Christ through bread and wine, affirmed that 'the Spirit truly unites things separated by space' – surely a comfort in this newly contactless life, where church reaches our kitchen via hagioscopic screens. Likewise, the Book of Common Prayer describes the 'heavenly and spiritual manner' of our bond, in which the infirm may partake, albeit remotely.

The Tocotes vault has sight of the altar, even though Sir Roger can no longer reach the rail. Encased as he is – and leprous with dates – he awaits the call to come out.

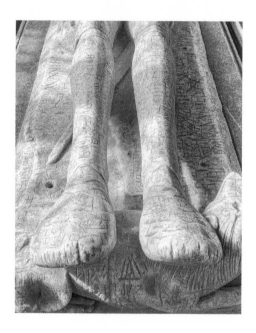

The rattling tree

Dawn along the Kennet valley, with a gloss of crows and the astringent echo of pheasants. Even, this morning, a barn owl: arcing the fence posts ahead of me like a beckoning spectre, milky against the hedgerow.

Job, in affliction, spoke of being 'a companion to owls' and such early excursions for the housebound have, likewise, found us mixing with birds – aware, perhaps for the first time, of their close, choral presence. Pre-Lockdown manoeuvres on Salisbury Plain in pursuit of the great bustard have triggered this also, and a pair of binoculars now stands sentry by the French window.

On Thursday morning, crossing the river at Clatford, I passed under a rattling tree: its arthritic limbs suddenly drummed into life. Pausing to record, I caught one tripling beat, before a fleeting slant of scarlet dropped down and away – a greater spotted woodpecker, I think. I have heard woodpeckers from afar before, but never directly underneath, or with such resonance and attack. It felt like an alarm, a report of spring. Arriving home, the clamour continued, reading the book of Ezekiel for a Passion Sunday sermon. Paired with the raising of Lazarus in St John's Gospel, this brace of weird, sinewy texts prepares the Church for what comes next – alerting the faithful to Lent's impending climax.

In a dream, the prophet is 'brought out by the spirit of the Lord' and set down in the middle of a valley full of dry bones. 'Mortal', the Lord questions him, 'can these bones live?', then commanding Ezekiel to prophesy to them, as it were to evoke God's hopeful future. 'And as I prophesied, suddenly there was a noise, a rattling, and the bones came together.' Like a scene from a gothic novel, skin and flesh renew each frame, and breath is summoned forth from the four winds. At each stage, it is Ezekiel (or 'mortal', as he is repeatedly addressed – the word hollow as an old oak) who must voice these remnants into being. As he does so, the whole, creaking multitude rises to its feet. Likewise, God tells Ezekiel, his exiled people will be convulsed into life by his Spirit – emerging from their graves to be placed on their own soil.

Like Tolkien's ents, the skeletal trees are stirring now, and softening with green – the scene and season reminding me to read (rather than skim for quotes, like much of my scavenging study) the Anglo-Saxon masterpiece *The Dream of the Rood*. This, the earliest English dream poem, transports its author to the edge of a mystic forest, 'where it seemed to me I saw the strangest of trees', dazzling and transfigured, which proceeds to speak of its unique conscription as the cross of Christ.

> Horror seized me when the hero clasped me,
> But I dared not bow or bend down to the earth,
> Nor falter, nor fall; firm I needs must stand.[10]

Red as a woodpecker's crest, the rood is stained, before its exaltation as the tree of triumph, berried with jewels. This vision ends with a charge: that the poet 'make manifest in words the mystery of the beam of glory'. Yet its recession leaves him newly rootless and alone on earth: unsatisfied on home soil and waiting only to be carried aloft to paradise – and there the cross, his soul's roost.

The fatal junction

Neck cricked back like a hammerhead – as if in ecstatic awe – and clad in a shelled shawl. Mallet held in one hand and, in the other, the figure grips a fecund branch, drawn down to his eye, close as a kiss.

Nowhere is this explained, so the cross at St Peter, Codford – one of the finest pieces of Anglo-Saxon stonework in England – is muted in its beauty. The dangling catkins may be those of an alder tree or, alternatively, the vine's produce envisaged in St John's Gospel: a motif of God's wayward people and of Christ, their fruitful stock. Others recognize the fertility god Sucellos and see this cross tangled with pagan imagery, like the Green Men gurning from parochial gutters.

Whatever it means, the pristine condition is what truly hits home, showing all the freshness and feel of an Arts and Crafts carving (especially the wayward chisel of Eric Gill) – a full millennium before that movement. We can see the vine dresser's curving calf, the line of his nose, the ridge and furrow landscape of his clothes. This is because the Codford cross was recovered from a recess inside the walls of St Peter's in the nineteenth century: a quiet anchorite, biding its time. From the immense patience of churches, it emerged into the chancel and now stands at the side like an uncertain communicant.

Most glaringly, it isn't a cross at all, just a stub or shaft, whose top section must yet be buried or bricked in hereabouts. And I can't decide quite how I feel about this elegant stem: about engraved women and men surrendering to spring's golden bough. I want to go with its grain, but also know my need of Easter's knot in the wood, Good Friday. To halt at its fatal junction, and find ourselves utterly blocked. Maybe it's the Passiontide mood, but life with the cross lopped off feels horrific – 'It is unfinished!' I want to cry.

Motoring home across Salisbury Plain from Codford, the A360 crosses the old Imber Road, now a restricted route for army vehicles on to their gunnery range. On the verge stands a stump of about the same size as the relic at St Peter's, known as The Robber's Stone. A kind of moral boundary marker, this commemorates the spot where a Mr Dean of Imber was attacked and robbed by four highwaymen, one October evening in 1839. 'After a spirited pursuit of three hours', it reads, 'one of the felons, Benjamin Colclough, fell dead on Chitterne Down', apparently having reached the cul-de-sac of his luck and strength.

The plaque was placed 'as a warning to those who presumptuously think to escape the punishment God has threatened against thieves and robbers': a monument, then, to merciless natural law. Two stones, Lenten signs, flanking Wiltshire's wilderness. I'm not sure which I would rather: limitless free will or the chill hand of justice. Neither, I think – for goodness alone knows how to traverse those lines.

The golden numbers

The elevated host of the paschal moon is spectral by six-thirty, a remote ghost over Avebury. It rarely lingers once the east colours with sunrise: burst yolk and rose pink, spreading softly, like ink through water.

'The Priest of Spring' by G. K. Chesterton – his finest essay in my opinion – begins by arraying 'two great armies of the human intellect who will fight to the end on this vital point, whether Easter is to be congratulated on fitting in with the Spring – or the Spring on fitting in with Easter'. Considering the sun, in particular, he contends that it is a blunder basic to modern thought to believe that the gods of ancient man were symbols of the sun, or moon – rather than the other way around. 'We human beings have never worshipped nature', he asserts – concluding, lyrically:

> And when I look across the sun-struck fields, I know in my inmost bones that my joy is not solely in the spring … [but] my pleasure is in some promise yet possible and in the resurrection of the dead.[11]

The close association of Christian and pagan celebrations marking nature's renewal – a mock battle re-enacted in the press like a festive cycle – is itself natural, and unless we hold that what came first is best (a slippery foothold for any cultural stance) the interesting thing is surely to consider their interrelation. For, as the social historian Keith Thomas (still publishing at the age of eighty-eight and whose contribution to this field is peerless) demonstrated in the twin works *Man and the Natural World* and *Religion and the Decline of Magic*,[12] our attitude and

action towards nature in this country has unquestion-
ably theological foundations. The demotion of nature in
Christianity's human-centred world view was, Thomas
writes, 'deeply ambivalent': sanctioning both its exploitation and yet providing the soil for compassionate
treatment of animals and the conviction – now, rightly,
to the fore – that creation is a sacred trust, and we its
custodians.

For Chesterton, 'when once a god is admitted, even a
false god, the cosmos begins to know its place: which is
second place', the paradox being that this lowering is, for
believers, the means of its exaltation, like a verse gaining
its glory from the chorus. In one sense Christian Easter
wraps itself around the natural year, as in the strange trig-
onometry of the Golden Numbers – that obscure (to me, at
least, however many times I attempt to unravel it) table at
the front of the 1662 Book of Common Prayer: buoyantly,
if needlessly, predicting the date of Easter until AD 8500.
Its 'ecclesiastical full moons' and other arcana suggest our
festival is entirely in tune with the music of the spheres.

But in another, crucial, sense Easter is wholly foreign:
no closer to a daffodil than the Dog Star. For the biblical
account of resurrection describes no iteration of a phe-
nomenon the world has already witnessed, but a startlingly
new creative act that, at one stroke, repositions everything
in its perspective. Faith that the rising of Christ has unique
gravity – greater even than that hauling the moon-washed
tides – can appear (and maybe is) deeply anthropocentric,
except that our forebears construed it also as the final
judgement of God upon all human hubris. And from this
root, every bud would erupt in full-leafed praise.

Sketches of the heavenly things

Ours is a life lived in response. Response, primarily, to our real situation and what it calls for, elicits from us. Existence stands at the door, knocking, and the truly life-changing moments (being the sphere of our greatest freedom and potential influence) are those in which we decide how to answer. Even when overcome or closed down by circumstance, this much remains open to us. Consequently, those who shape life most profoundly – who, for good or ill, end up forging the reality the rest of us reckon with – tend to be those who are most responsive, or responsible. Who, like Moses before the bush, consider themselves addressed by the fearful brilliance of what *is*.

Attention to each particular locus is thus the key to a creative life. I read this week that John Constable, recalling the first stirrings of an artistic vocation, wrote how 'the trees seemed to ask me to try and do something like them' – his experience, in other words, required some kind of reply. What we name as self-possession is really our possession of just this: our own unique answer – and, in realizing this liberty, each of us makes the world anew.

That recognition, taken one way, can lead towards the exaltation of genius advocated by Ralph Waldo Emerson in his renowned essay 'Self-Reliance': 'Insist on yourself: never imitate.' The best part of his case concerns human timidity before the present moment. We are, he repines:

ashamed before the blade of grass or the blowing rose. These roses under my window make no reference to former roses or to better ones; they are for what they are; they exist with God today. There is no time to them.

There is simply the rose; it is perfect in every moment of its existence. Before a leaf-bud has burst, its whole life acts ...[13]

What he gains in elevating personal agency Emerson loses, however, by painting himself into an individualist corner, where everyone is an island. 'Is not a man better than a town?' he concludes, in humourless antithesis to John Donne.

The genius of Christ (which Emerson admits among those uniquely able to command a cause) points another way. What makes all that came before him mere 'sketches of the heavenly things', as the writer of the Epistle to the Hebrews puts it, is really the nature, the quality of his response – as though God himself were owning the questions of existence that spring from its compound of barbarism and beauty. The Passion has captivated art, partly because, with every tightening fetter, Christ retains this capacity for responding as we might, but cannot. He is life's advocate, even in the rasps of Golgotha.

Like Constable's tree, the cross thus arrests our attention, that we may approximate something like it. The resurrection is another matter entirely – beyond our palette, reason or reply. And not an answer, as such – more a dazzling, dumbfounding rejoinder: *What will you make of this?*

A time of grave emergency

Do not be astonished at this; for the hour is coming
when all who are in their graves will hear his voice and
will come out ...
John 5.28–29

Dawn walks have lately become my liturgy: a faithful
repetition. The same circuit of fields and lanes, nature's
performance framing days that are improvisations on a
theme. Mundane though it is to do the same old thing, or
view a constant scene, we become attuned to small alter-
ations in self or situation that would otherwise have no
measure. As Dietrich Bonhoeffer wrote from his Berlin
prison in May 1944:

> Where the ground bass is firm and clear, there is nothing
> to stop the counterpoint from being developed to the
> utmost of its limits.[14]

This work of walking has provided the *cantus firmus* for
Lockdown, my metronome feet beating the bounds, keeping pace with events. Today's tableau has changed again:
last time I passed, the sun hung in this tree like a bauble;
this morning it is offset, a soft bulb, while the leaves jiggle
like bunting.

If resurrection is, as Christ imagined, something that is
wrought from the earth, the clues to which surround us,
then perhaps we shouldn't be astonished if those in whose
steps we tread reappear along the way. It being the VE
Day anniversary, my late father is beside me, especially,
and at home I recover from his papers the demobilization

43

letter sent from the War Office in September 1946. Like countless others, rapped out on a Remington, its repeated form ('the valuable services you have rendered in service of your country at a time of grave national emergency', 'I am, Sir, your obedient servant ...') undergirds rather than undermines the particular, personal case – implying as it does that solo efforts belonged in a symphony of service and were not lost in that clamour. The letter has, at some point, been prised from a frame: there is a rough, gluey border that proves its value – surprising to me, as such things were never displayed at home.

From India, where he served with the Royal Engineers, Dad was brought at the end of the war to Berlin, by rumbling Liberator bomber. For several months, he took part in the allied recovery operation among these flattened cities – clearing the rubble of Hamburg, Hanover and Essen. Something of their desolation awakened his own and, unforeseen, he stumbled into personal crisis. His mother (lost to him when a few months old) and father – always remote, but recently departed – rose, as it were, in grief's pale disguise. As for most of us, all that had been lost remained, of all things, acutely present.

The apparition was an unwanted gift, but a gift nonetheless. My father's 'deep problems' (as he described them) were redeemed as the seam of a compassionate parish ministry, but reprised in retirement. Keenly I recall praying, as he preached from some Herefordshire pulpit, that the good Lord would help it to end well. For it was in stillness – waiting on appointments with God – that he was renewed and where he 'reposed, in conscious weakness', as one of his favourite divines, Bishop Handley Moule, put it. Soon after Dad died, I wrote a scrap of a poem that I had thought was about me, but now see was entirely him:

That which you lack
will draw you back
to where the silence sings.
The yawning gape,
the ache
and crack
become a place
of springs.

The South Cerney Christ

Resurrection at South Cerney. A massive medieval tomb chest, eight inches thick, its lifted lid cracked about the neckline and propped, as if in an Easter garden, all moss and enormous narcissi. This gaping, vacant bath, close by the south door – as if to broadcast 'he is not here' – arrests any visitor, suggesting its occupant may be found wandering in bandages about the graveyard, puzzled as to why night still falls in the realms of endless day.

I am staying up the road at the Cotswold Water Park, a vast archipelago of lakes (147 in all) created in the 1990s from limestone gravel pits. It's an oddly anonymous community for the countless clapboard homes that have spread like reed beds around the periphery, although that suits me on a day's retreat – planning the new season, gazing at grebes and kayaks.

The ancient village of South Cerney ('Saxon Parish, Charter AD 999' capitalizes the sign) has been somewhat swamped by this convenient Venice, yet offers the resort an anchor in deep time and place. Inside All Hallows Church, red and white incident tape decorates the pew ends, although nothing seems to have occurred. Like many, I enjoy being alone in churches and, were I not ordained to lead, would be one of those slipping into Evensong along the back pew – with a smile at the door, but little chat.

An illuminated recess in the chancel holds a resin replica (the original sits in the British Museum) of the twelfth-century South Cerney Christ – the oldest wooden crucifix in the country and the only such relic of Romanesque art. Rescued from a long-felled rood screen, then entombed in a wall chamber to evade destruction, only the head and one nail-pocked foot were found – during renovations, in 1912. While the corpus may have been consumed by beetles (evidence of a 1,000-year-old wood-boring insect has been detected) the face remains serenely intact.

By the time South Cerney received from Aethelred the Unready its charter, England (or 'Engla-lond' as it would have been) was at last a definable kingdom. Having begun as what Robert Tombs has called 'a hypothetical nation', a religious idea that preceded reality, the Anglo-Saxon achievement (albeit over five centuries) was arguably to find a workable balance between local, national and global identities. At the end of the first millennium, Cerney, England and Christendom were, in effect, different scales of the same thing.

This may appear unremarkable before noticing how confoundingly hard we find it to do likewise in the present day. The relationship between particular and universal – the axis of philosophy since Aristotle – is subtle, personal and precisely what is tying British society in knots. The figure of Christ embodies this conundrum, being both genius of another place entirely and so deeply buried within our culture that he might disintegrate.

Five hundred hands high

A gauzy sky, veiling the sun, but the kind of April afternoon when spring seems unstoppable: the countryside
bridal in its beauty and promise. A giddy, elevating day,
so I stray off the main road and up a thin strap of lane
hung like a stirrup from Westbury Hill.

An emblematic white horse – oldest and largest of the
Wiltshire hill figures – has grazed here for centuries, though
no one knows quite how many. Like the charts of equine
evolution I remember from childhood (*mesohippus*, *mery-
chippus*, *equus*, ran the incantation, toes turning to hooves
with every metrical foot), the Westbury horse has changed
in size and appearance across time, though somewhat less
imaginatively at each stage. While the current breed ('a
moderately correct, dispirited animal' sniffs Pevsner, who
has a point) has clearly been broken in, an engraving from
the eighteenth century shows its eccentric predecessor
facing the opposite direction. An animated mount, with
a single, antic eye and unlikely swirling fishtail, this beast
came from somewhere else entirely – perhaps the primeval
sea that once covered the plain hereabouts. When the
Psalms declare 'an horse is a vain thing for safety' this,
you feel, was closer to the spirit they had in mind.

Where the Westbury horse impresses, however, is in
sheer scale and landmark visibility: 180 feet tall and view-
able from Bath. Concealed with scrub during World War
Two to confuse enemy bomb-aimers – then, in peacetime,
periodically illuminated by army searchlights, just for the
spectacle. 'Art is the signature of man', wrote Chesterton,
weighing the human desire to reflect and depict their fellow
creatures. Alone among animals, he continued, we have 'a

mind like a mirror ... because in it all the other shapes can be seen like shining shadows in a vision'.

Soil erosion and rainfall mean that chalk horses soon become grey, dun and dappled, requiring a surprising amount of livery. Hence the pleasingly municipal post-war decision to concrete the Westbury horse in place (one wonders how many other challenges faced by the Council in the 1950s met with a similar response), so that it would simply want occasional whitewashing. However sensible, this pan stick somehow renders it static: a stuccoed steed, needing to shake free a little.

And riding above, the intense, buffeting quiet of high places: a stony car park and skylark's trilling signal. Bratton Camp embosses the ground here: a formidable Iron Age fort that may mark the site of King Alfred's great victory at Ethandun, which the original chalk figure is thought to commemorate. Far beneath this tattoo, a pair of miniature white horses, displayed in the pasture as souvenirs.

Hard sentences

Verging the A4, walking west and nature everywhere in debut. Limp rotors of horse chestnut leaf, ear-handles of lambs, sweetly outsized and sooty: the year is taking shape but still untested, tentative. Wild Chervil, which will flock this path shortly, has a shyness in unfurling. Its fronds first genuflect, before an ecstatic flowering into tiny white explosions – flung out yet restrained, on stems taut as fuse wire.

Life thus reins us in, even in spring. Wendell Berry, in his essay 'The Work of Local Culture', describes the containment necessary for an ecology to thrive: 'the growth of the years must return – or be returned – to the ground to rot and build soil.' This return applies as much to human society as agriculture, as Berry continues:

> A human community, then, if it is to last long, must exert a kind of centripetal force, holding local soil and local memory in place.[15]

The dominant force in modern, urban culture is, he argues, centrifugal – and Berry looks askance at its cancerous expansion – 'eating its way outwards, like ringworm'. Wendell Berry is a writer of singular genius, whose grounded Christian ethic has grown from a lifetime of farming the same Kentucky acres. His gift is to see human and natural culture as an organic whole, a spiritual compact – encapsulated by 'culture' itself, whose root words hold in tension the sense of natural growth and husbandry, Adamic delving in the soil (as in *coulter*, or ploughshare) and, tellingly, the honouring with worship still evident in our use of *cult*.

Traditional agricultural communities shackled most members to the soil with a toiling gravity still present when my mother began teaching in Lincolnshire villages in the late 1940s. Stone-picking and other, equally back-breaking tasks tugged pupils to the fields, bringing mass seasonal absence. Industrialization and its corollaries burst these communities like a seed head, scattering labouring classes into the towns and leaving those who remained oddly shiftless – unless, like my grandfather, they too mechanized and mobilized.

Modernity's mistake was to dupe us into believing we could liberate ourselves from the natural world and still flourish: a lesson we are having to relearn now – in 'hard sentences', as the Psalms put it. We cannot contract out of our skin or away from the soil, although culture always changes, as each paradigm drifts. Having lived with high personal mobility and low remote connection, we are now hastened into the opposite – broadcast beyond recognition, but at the same time rooted anew in one place, schooled again in the names of the creation, like children of Eve. Our footing, for now, is hesitant: lamb-like, yet hefting with every step.

In terra pax

May breaks, with a complex sky and high procession of clouds. Earth is mobile, mercurial – mirroring the heavens, like the cold sun of each spent dandelion. Simone Weil, a writer whose lightning insights smoulder still, considered this counterpoint to be more than merely material:

> Every human being has at their roots here below a certain terrestrial poetry, a reflection of the heavenly glory, the link, of which they are more or less vaguely conscious, with their universal country.

That our shifting, temporal existence might be partnered in a dance with eternity is an idea old as wisdom, and has choreographed the Christian understanding of space and time. Our 'terrestrial poetry' plots this instinct, requiring 'you are here' arrows to indicate the way. Even the most outlandish scriptural depictions of the next world are necessarily rooted in this one (St John's apocalyptic monsters still have wings and eyes, even if uncannily numerous) – the biblical heaven, in other words, is an extrapolation of the biblical earth.

A church spire is thus an upended map pin: a stake in empyrean fields, as if our mortal tent could swiftly blow away. In a week when many were due to gather for the 800th anniversary of Salisbury Cathedral's foundation, this is much in mind. I am carried back to a service there on this date last year, for the installation of new honorary canons – an event as ethereal as any I can recall. The atmosphere inside was seraphic, as we wafted on soft voluntaries to fill, among others, the vacant prebendary stalls of Alton Borealis and Netherbury in Terra.

My initial response was entirely to these radiant names: imagined and alternative versions of ordinary diocesan villages. *Where on earth are these places?* Viewed one way, this was obscure ceremonial with roundly earthbound roots: prebends had been valuable endowments of land or other revenue attached to the office of cathedral canon and thereby prone to becoming the ecclesiastical equivalent of rotten boroughs. Yet the effect of invoking them was tremendous and, by the conclusion of worship, I felt as if we had visited another dimension, in which familiar parishes each had their celestial counterpart. Wherever Alton Borealis is, I felt, I want to dwell there.

From Martinsell – Iron Age hillfort and one of the loftiest, as well as most peaceful spots in Wiltshire – you can, on a clear day, see across Salisbury Plain to where the foremost spire in England lances the skies, glorifying God in the highest. It remains a kind of eternal trig point for pilgrims, including Thomas Fuller, an army chaplain from the English Civil War ('A good Church of England man, with his heart in heaven and both feet on the ground', according to one commentator). In his memoir of those stricken years, *Mixt Contemplations*, he reflects:

> Travelling on the plain (which notwithstanding hath its risings and fallings) I discovered Salisbury steeple many miles off; coming to a declivity, I lost sight thereof; but climbing up on the next hill, the steeple grew out of the ground again. Yea, I often found it and lost it, till at last I came safely to it, and took my lodging near it. It fareth thus with us while we are wayfaring to heaven. Mounted on the Pisgah top of some good meditation, we get a glimpse of our celestial Canaan; but when on the flat of an ordinary temper, or in the fall of an extraordinary temptation, we lose the view thereof. Thus, in the sight of our souls, heaven is discovered, covered, and recovered; till – though late, at last – though slowly, surely – we arrive at the haven of our happiness.[16]

Super flumina

Sideburns of cow parsley bushing into the lane, you lean into the corners like Moss, Hawthorn or Hill: all those racing drivers with hedgerow names. Spring means motoring by faith, not by sight.

I am due at Pewsey Wharf for the final leg of a fundraising walk, organized by Christian Aid. Over four days they have toured the Wiltshire white horses, finishing with the smallest – a modest pair of foals at Marlborough and Pewsey. Happily, it begins along the Kennet and Avon canal that veins west across the county from Reading. Blue on the map, brown on the land: a scratch or scar, unhurriedly scored into Wessex between 1724 and 1810. The notorious chain of locks at Caen Hill was the last stretch to be built – a staggering staircase of twenty-nine, over two miles. It takes a full day to fall 237 feet through their yawning doors, but this still made the Kennet and Avon – part canal, part navigable river – faster to Bath than the stagecoach. The age of acceleration was beginning: just yards from the towpath lance the dark-green Hitachi trains of the Great Western Railway, following the line sketched by Brunel as he trudged these fields with his theodolite.

There is nothing you could call a current here – just a slight drift, reflecting the landscape in sepia. Symmetrical trees, seen through this silted filter; the rippling reply of your boots under each bridge: the canal is a constant commentary, a gloss on the usual paths. The dogged redigging of our inland waterways – half a century of voluntary spadework – has been an immense unearthing, the purpose of which is interesting to ponder. Was it radical or reactionary? Alternative or conservative? Any such recovery is a social critique: seeking to reclaim something lost or denied. To abide by the water, like the rope-bound homes along this reach, involves a conscious step aside from progress.

The Vale of Pewsey embodies these views, these tensions. Parliamentarian in the English Civil War, Wiltshire was considered pivotal for the Royalist cause, and the Battles of Marlborough and Roundway Down were fought nearby – the former being reclaimed for the king in 1642. The walls of St Mary's Church in Marlborough are still musket-pocked from the conflict.

William Cobbett, one of my co-walkers informs me, passed through Pewsey on his polemical tour of agricultural conditions, written up as *Rural Rides*. 'In taking my leave of this beautiful vale', commented Cobbett in 1826, 'I have to express my deep shame, as an Englishman, at beholding the general extreme poverty of those who cause this vale to produce such quantities of food and raiment. This is, I verily believe it, the *worst used labouring people upon the face of the earth*. Dogs and hogs and horses are treated with *more civility*.'[17] Unsurprising, then, that four years later his simmering valley became the county's flashpoint for the Swing riots – when farm workers, like Samson's foxes, set torches to the hayricks and destroyed the threshing machines, loathed for their labour-saving innovation.

This is a resistant landscape. Looping away from the walk, I pass back through Pewsey village, pausing to snoop in a collapsing barn often sighted from the road. Astonishingly, among the rusting seed drills stands an abandoned nineteenth-century haywain, parked like a protest against time.

The rutted path

Thou shalt not remove thy neighbour's landmark.
Deuteronomy 19.14

May is the abundant month: her bounties come in showers.
Overpowering mists of hawthorn blossom, elegant cranes
of buttercups: uplifted nature's open hand. And, in the
coming days, Rogationtide – when, by ancient custom,
parish bounds are beaten and (in those tracks) the waxing

crops are blessed. A time to consider the benefit of this particular plot: the yield of the season.

From Overton Hill, walking north along the Ridgeway, I am also tracing a parish boundary. Often following more ancient patterns, these frequently picked up hitchhiking landmarks – long barrows, especially – incorporating them to delimit parochial or manorial lands. In her exploration of England's 'spiritual topography', *Inhabiting the Landscape*,[18] the historian Nicola Whyte demonstrates how a range of Christian and pre-Christian territorial markers – standing crosses, for example – linked with natural features to form a 'mnemonic' framework that enabled communities to learn their locale by heart. Perhaps inevitably, these lines also symbolized the threshold between life and death: burial mounds in some cases becoming sites of a gallows or gibbet, usually at a conjunction of routes.

Pausing at the Ridgeway's intersection with the 'Herepath' or Green Street (another prehistoric trackway), the crops look ripe for a reading of the 103rd Psalm, one of the customary Rogationtide texts. Since I last visited, a lush velour of barley has covered these crusted furrows – the brown sweep of the fields now furred by a soft green pelt. The 'perambulation' of parish bounds in this season was, interestingly, the only outdoor religious procession to survive the English Reformation: not simply permitted but mandated by the Injunctions of Henry VIII and Elizabeth I. While this accords with the growing significance of the parish as the footing for local government (whose powers accrued for a further three centuries), attachment to the enchanted landmarks of Catholic – and, indeed, pagan – practice persisted, only being dislocated by the ever-expanding privatization and enclosure of common ground.

For a thousand years, these ceremonies defined community as a triangular conversation between God, land and humanity, with Scripture employed as the mediating language of our dialogue with nature. In this, it was both the term of address – William Tyndale describes the 'saying of gospels to the corn in the procession week, that it should better grow' – and also of reply, for the same Gospel would be read from holy trees (hence 'Gospel Oak'), that those gathered should likewise flourish. In a roughly practical outworking (Rogationtide processions could also be the riotous flashpoint for disputation with neighbours), the words of the Bible thus sealed our covenant with the soil.

That is a compact worth renewing as we land from modernity's long-haul flight, and reckon again with the routes of community. So today, I pray from the rutted path: with suede-faced fallow deer and fly-twitched cattle; with rosters of red campion and bush vetch, and a skylark to cantor the wind's amen.

Lively stones

To sit alone in a country church is companionable solitude: a volume of silence. I am at St Michael's, Tidcombe, prior to taking a service for its rededication next weekend: writing my sermon in the church seemed appropriate and ought, I thought, allow the place to permeate my words a little. Major repairs to these lively stones were being undertaken, following a heroic fundraising effort – then, as happens in so many similar cases, thieves arrived by night and used the scaffolding to remove lead from the roof, rolling it up in heavy carpets, carting it away through the graveyard.

Such ruinous seasons of metal theft – sometimes being inflicted multiple times on the same church – are almost beyond endurance for those already shouldering the massive cost of our built heritage. The Church of England looks after a startling 45 per cent of all Grade I listed buildings in the country, and each one has to be sustained by voluntary effort – often by tiny communities, as in Tidcombe. So it is an amazing, praiseworthy feat that the majority of England's 15,700 parish churches are in such good shape and a defiant sign of life that St Michael's has a gleaming new roof (this time, in terne-coated stainless steel).

Church buildings run by subtle semiotics, always signifying something just out of sight. *Underneath*, reads a tombstone – the word embellished for emphasis – 'are deposited the mortal remains of Edward Tanner, many years an inhabitant of this parish'. Rustily caged, an enclosure for creatures long departed, the monument points to what is beyond and invites you to imagine it, grisly or glorious. Because they express investment in what cannot be seen (barely even articulated), these emblems are potent beyond belief. We are unable to grasp the thing signified, so the physical sign becomes a vital proxy. This instinct can, of course, be baneful (as any parish priest knows), but to suppress or ignore it is folly, for it can also point us to paradise.

The font in Tidcombe Church is a fine example. Perhaps because it doesn't belong to anyone in particular – but thousands of lives, fondly or briskly christened – its personal significance is both diffused and amplified. In buttery limestone, faintly striated, it is a deep and beautiful thing – thought to be Saxon and to date from around AD 850. Being so soaked in association – with bawling, aspirant life, and the Christ of this place – the St Michael's font fairly pulses.

We can no more evacuate divine meaning from the material world as live in the clouds. This is why we shall continue to replace the church roof and thermometer our appeals to heaven. My sermon complete, I sketch the font in 6B, enjoy a silent sandwich, then leave.

Out of the cloudy pillar

'For the healthy visionary,' writes Aldous Huxley in *Heaven and Hell*, 'the perception of the infinite in the finite particular is a revelation of divine immanence.'[19] Unassisted by mescaline (this morning being hazy enough), I'm off and away by six or so, searching for what Huxley calls 'the union with divine ground'.

Ascension Day is an inspiring space in the Anglican calendar. The departure of Christ – 'carried up into heaven' – is, in the fullest sense, an imaginary thing, in which the elastic of language is stretched tight before snapping back to earth, as all language must. St Luke attests that 'a cloud received him out of their sight', and out of sight means that in our mind we must now conceive him. It is not simply that all talk of God must use analogy, but – as Dorothy L. Sayers explains – that 'all language about everything is analogical' – not being the thing itself, but a limited descriptor. She continues:

> To complain that man measures God by his own experience is a waste of time; man measures everything by his own experience; he has no other yardstick.[20]

So what if we experience – as we regularly do – something beyond words: what, then, can we say? We speak of elevated or 'heightened' language to convey our sense of a reality beyond our ken, that nonetheless meets us and invites that we reframe our referents. This is what Huxley, discussing the heavenly vision in art, meant by 'the impossible paradox and supreme truth – that perception is (or at least can be, ought to be) the same as Revelation ...' All truly new experience has this quality, in which we realize life, not as a monologue but an antiphon, responding to prior reality – the word that was in the beginning.

The most novel encounters or experiences appear to go ahead of us, like the fiery, cloudy pillar before the children of Israel – and really require a new kind of tense, for they seem to come from past and future simultaneously. The closest English word for this convergence is 'before' – meaning both 'previously' and 'ahead of'. As Jesus explains to the Twelve what could never be anticipated, he says: 'after I am risen again, I will go *before* you into Galilee.'

The language of God always goes first. The resurrection and ascension as described in Scripture are not so much 'what happened' as an inspired bid to express what was inherently inexpressible, by virtue of being entirely new. The old words wouldn't quite do. Thus we must settle for heaven above and earth below, although an intersection of the two is where we reside in this rapturous season, suspended like those of whom St Paul writes, 'which are alive and remain [who] shall be caught up together ... to meet the Lord in the air'.

Looking up, the firmament is flocked. Clouds crowd the sunlight, leaving the land baffled.

Safernoc

The midst of May: nature's parade. My son, mock-revising (and himself a biological marvel, inching ever upwards to the sun), enthuses at the brilliance of plants – every leaf a factory at peak, puffing out its perfect equation of elements.

This photosynthetic month is ideal for discovering the Savernake – seven square miles of antique woodland and perhaps our most precious scrap of primeval forest. Hitherto, my encounters with this enchanted plateau have been limited to rushing through the verdant corridor of the A346 on my way to Salisbury: dodging cadavers of deer and the portly tangle of the Big Belly Oak, reputedly the nation's oldest. This behemoth is thought to be 1,100 years old, having cracked through its acorn when the Anglo-Saxon kingdoms finally united under King Athelstan, in whose annals the forest is first recorded – as 'Safernoc'. Like a snarling cyclops, restrained by a steel collar to prevent it collapsing (or running amok), the Big Belly is an icon of England, and roughly the same vintage. Its shock of leaves in spring brings to mind a line from George Herbert: 'who would have thought my shrivel'd heart could have recover'd greenness?'[21]

Today, though, I am drawn deeper in – through the trees to a chapel of ease: St Katharine's Church, perched like a nesting box in the north-eastern branches of the forest. This pocket cathedral, consecrated in 1861, is a woodland glade in stone, sharing the Savernake's spirit of stilled anticipation: as if before the starting pistol. When, at the end of World War Two, an ammunition store hidden close by exploded, nearly every window was blasted out and the walls so badly weakened that a diocesan committee suggested St Katharine's be demolished. Yet here she remains, unshattered.

Red-bricked relics in various stages of decay decorate the lanes hereabouts: the former Forest Hotel, whose last guests left in the late 1990s, remnants of the high- and low-level rail stations (the platform of the former now a sunken garden) and corroded gateways to absent avenues. The Savernake has stayed privately owned since 1548, when granted to the Seymour family of Wolf Hall – favoured as a hunting lodge by Henry VIII when pursuing his dubious quarry. Although the original hall wasted away soon after that other obese oak, a sole stained window was recovered and illuminates Great Bedwyn Church, all Tudor flowers and faded feathers. Hilary Mantel's dazzling novels have sparked such interest in the site that the current, crumbling pile at Wolfhall Farm now bristles with archaeologists. I watched them briefly: waist deep in the Seymour sewer system, brushing off the rock of ages.

At its largest extent in the thirteenth century, the Saver-nake Forest covered an area ten times its present patch – reaching to Hungerford in the east and south nearly as far as Salisbury Plain – becoming so large that, in order to prevent it merging with the other eight Wiltshire forests into one arboreal conurbation, two clauses in the Magna Carta were needed explicitly to limit its spread. By the time Capability Brown arranged his scheme of radial parades and pleasing bowers, the forest had been pollarded down to pretty much its present size.

A very human wilderness, then. Yet wild it is, never-theless – and if men and women withdrew, an unbound Savernake would soon reclaim whatever ground has been lost. Its oldest oaks provoke an awe bordering on fear, certainly. Strolling up Long Harry – a path worth walking for the name alone – I approach the Cathedral Oak, a spreading millennial with a hide like Dürer's rhinoceros. Before its chancel of branches you can either stand, trans-fixed, or slowly retreat.

Above the verbing stream

One day telleth another; and one night certifieth another.
There is neither speech nor language; but their voices are
heard among them.
Psalm 19.2–3

The River Kennet is a chattering baptism of accents. Its
ceaseless issue of conversation (with brisk reeds and mute
rocks) chortles and gasps like a passing circle of intimates.
Propped on a breezy footbridge, one among the thousand tongues, I mutter along with nature's praise: today's
acceptable sacrifice.

None of us knows how to pray as we ought, St Paul
consolingly writes to the Romans. The Spirit – articu-
late gust of life – intercedes for us with sighs too deep
for words. Perhaps, then, our first lesson in prayer is that
we are each mute as Zechariahs before God, lacking the
river's fluency. Only then must we open our lips, for him
to fill our emptiness: only then can we bless the Pente-
costal wind.

In the days of Abbess Hilda of Whitby, in AD 680, The
Venerable Bede tells us there lived one 'whom God's grace
made remarkable': Caedmon, our country's first named
poet. Caedmon could, apparently, conduct words like
notes – composing 'whatever passages of Scripture were
explained to him into delightful and moving poetry in his
own English tongue'. This translation, from the regiments
of Latin to the ill-disciplined spells of England, spilled over
from Caedmon's initial admission that he had nothing
whatsoever to say before heaven.

The tale is told that, at feasts, when guests turned to entertain one another with song and the harp passed, terrifyingly, to him, Caedmon would rise and leave. After one such exit, hot-faced and alone, he fell asleep in a stable – only to meet, in a dream, a figure who asks Caedmon to sing him a song. To his reply that he can't sing – that was why he left the feast – the visitor insists, more as a promise than a threat, 'But you shall sing to me.' Caedmon (flailing by this point) asks, helplessly, 'What should I sing about?' 'Sing about the creation of all things', comes the angelic answer – and Bede tells how, immediately, Caedmon's hymn commenced:

> Now we ought to praise the Guardian of the heavenly
>   kingdom,
> The might of the Creator and his conception,
> The work of the glorious Father, as he of each of the
>   wonders,
> Eternal Lord, established the beginning.
> He first created for the sons of men
> Heaven as a roof, holy Creator;
> Then the middle-earth, the Guardian of mankind,
> The eternal Lord, afterwards made
> The earth for men, the Lord almighty.

Bede adds, endearingly, that this is only the gist – and loses the lyrical beauty that became Caedmon's trademark. Thereafter a brother in the Whitby community, he died, we learn, yet uttering praise, until his tongue was stilled again before the throne of grace. Translating nature's speechless psalms is the poetic task – and a vocation, in Caedmon's case. If the people remain silent, Christ said, the very rocks will cry out. I shall wait, then, for quiet interpretation, above the verbing stream.

Room for abysses

Avebury at dawn: commuting cars slalom the sarsens. Sheep nibble their perimeter and cattle slump beside them, amid the mingling village that has encroached in pocks and patches, like lichen. Such accessibility is what makes this a far more beguiling landmark than Stonehenge, twenty-five miles to the south. Unlike its famous neighbour, isolated on the plain, Avebury is an interrupted circuit: arcane geometry confused and bisected by succeeding centuries. The High Street intrudes like a radius and the parish church of St James sits, it seems, at a deliberate tangent.

Certainly, the world's largest megalithic circle is contested territory. The number of standing stones has been decimated from the hundred or so originally planted, many having been re-employed in the walls of local houses or farm buildings. Had it not been for the careful work of two antiquarians, John Aubrey (1626–97) and the Reverend William Stukeley (1687–1765), who sketched, studied, and publicized the site, what remains might also have been blasted into rubble. Some were doubtless toppled by mis-placed Christian zeal, but the worst destructions, in the early eighteenth century, appear to have been far more mundane – with Stukeley recording:

> Just before I visited this place ... the inhabitants were fallen into the custom of demolishing the stones, chiefly out of covetousness of the little area of ground, each stood on.

Noting the lengths to which villagers would go to under-mine and obliterate the rocks, Stukeley observed them lighting great straw fires beneath, before attacking the brittle blocks with hammers, 'which has made most miserable havock of this famous temple'. An improbable twentieth-century saviour appeared in Alexander Keiller, the 'marmalade millionaire', whose family genius for pre-serving extended to his purchase of the Avebury Manor and stones in the 1930s. The resulting restoration – and subsequent sale to the National Trust – remains conten-tious, owing to Keiller's gradual displacement of homes lying within the circle to the nearby hamlet of Avebury Trusloe.

Our rearrangement of history comes in waves: each justifiable in its way, but often with monumental presump-tion. Unlike the heavenly mansions imagined by Jesus, our dwelling on the past is not often roomy, especially when it overlooks our 'little area of ground'. But the dyke around Avebury was not intended to be defensive: its purpose, so far as we can tell, was to enfold divine worship. The false stubs and absent teeth in this gigantic maw tell its story more truthfully than any restorative bridgework could do. And the fine efforts recently – not least by the parish priest – in cultivating peaceable conversation between the village's competing traditions thankfully indicates a less entrenched future.

At this summer's estranged solstice, there may be more accommodation than we think. 'Even great faith leaves room for abysses', wrote Elizabeth Jennings – and in these voids of our unknowing, we meet.

Groans of the Britons

The Bath Road verge is, by June, virtually impassable. All the infant weeds that played about my ankles in April are now five feet high, jostling me as I push through. Tallest of all, giant hogweed can double that height and is, I find, quite beautiful in tone and form – if also fearsomely harmful. Its sap can burn like ammonia, so it pays to be watchful when brushing past.

A caustic mood is scorching the land. We are wounded, aggrieved: immediate in our need and unsure of the ground, before or ahead. On my mind for days has been a Bible passage from the Anglican lectionary: Deuteronomy 8, verse 2. 'Remember the long way that the LORD your God has led you these forty years in the wilderness ... testing you to know what was in your heart ...' Remember the long way. I have been reading Anglo-Saxon history in the evenings, scouting the dark forest of English beginnings, lit by occasional glades (a Gildas here, a Bede there) to guide the way. Unifying the nation then was an arduous business: obscure centuries of conflict and toil before British, Germanic and Danish races integrated under the same monarch, faith and tongue.

Notwithstanding the bias of contemporary chroniclers, it may be no exaggeration to claim that the main agent of this gradual movement was the Christian Church that, in Peter Hunter Blair's words, had the capacity 'to act as a unit in a country where political unity did not yet exist'.[22] By a fairly unassailable blend of administrative nous, monastic incubation of learning and creative arts and a new, unifying social ethic, the Gregorian vision that impelled Augustine to the Kent coast – that of a single

73

English people under God – became a self-organizing reality. Within a century, the Church had become the indispensable secretariat to the regional kingdoms: referee to each game of thrones.

Crucially, too, it was Christians who told the long story – for they could write. Weaving biblical narrative into the national scene, the monk Gildas described the island of Britain as 'poised in the divine balance, which supports the whole world' – as if it were the axis of history. Writing in the sixth century, as the receding legions left the Isles floundering against invasion, he describes how 'a wretched remnant' made a final, unheeded appeal to the Roman consul for help, headed 'the groans of the Britons'. Whether or not Rome's eventual return to England – as Christendom, rather than empire – was a prayer answered, it bound Church and state in a knot we have yet to unravel.

If the nation still groans, the Church must groan with it. But in what voice? Such power as the Anglican Church retains is a curiosity to most and an offence to some: vestigial and deeply anachronistic. Artistic patronage and civil service long since shed, the last part (and the best, arguably) of the Anglo-Saxon body politic that this Church may yet recover is the power of speech – a ministry of the word.

National memory is ever selective, as we are realizing anew: always marshals the facts in order to tell a better story. Bede's *Ecclesiastical History* was, famously, not a history of the Church, but of the English people, from the Church's perspective. How to view the country's past is a tale that could usefully be told by an old institution, especially when we go to seed. Unlikely or archaic, these could be memories with a future.

The old eternal rocks

On Monday a friend from London called: passing through Marlborough to visit his mother. Jim suggested strolling to Devil's Den, an imposing dolmen now the only remnant of a Neolithic long barrow that, tantalizingly, could still be seen a century ago – extending back, like a leg under a blanket. Subsequently levelled by ploughing apparently – although this is hard to countenance, given the interest in such places by then. The main clue to its reformation is an etched date – 1921 – in a slab propping up the two that act as pallbearers to a hulking seventeen-ton capstone, which hangs impossibly in the air.

This idea of a raised, 'hanging' stone is one possible origin of the word 'henge', which first appears in the twelfth-century *Historia Anglorum* of Henry, Archdeacon of Huntingdon, in his listing of 'Stanenges' as the second of his four wonders of England. The conjuring feat that elevated Devil's Den is certainly wondrous and, to me, uncanny, being an embodiment of a perplexing dream I have experienced since childhood (whenever running a fever): of a colossal boulder oddly made light.

Jim and I don't often meet, but conversation runs easily and enjoyably deep when we do. It is four weeks since I have walked this way and already the track is unrecognizable. Soft spurs of toadflax, purple puffs of scabious have grown on the bank, alongside several others I can't identify. Everything has developed that sketchy, overgrown fringe midsummer brings to the countryside, and I find myself feeling neglectful of this familiar path – ridiculously, almost hurt that it has progressed without me.

But nature has no lasting city and there is consolation in

time's ceaseless passage, as with all things entirely beyond our control. This is why, I think, we find the coast so restful – marking as it does the limit of each territorial conquest. The early chroniclers of our national life were only too conscious of this – indeed, repeated waves of invasion were often the cue for their histories, which invariably sought to interpret successive calamities within the will and judgement of God. For a thousand years, from Gildas to Milton (whose *History of Britain*, written in 1670, is really the last of these), English history considered the tide of our affairs as though it were an extension of the book of Kings – weighing human hubris against divine piety.

Henry of Huntingdon's famous account of King Cnut is emblematic of this – and of personal interest to me, given that one of my forebears as Bishop of Ramsbury, St Bertwald, was reputedly that monarch's close political adviser. I imagine him by the shore, wondering what on earth to say. 'At the height of his ascendancy', Henry writes:

> [Cnut] ordered his chair to be placed on the sea-shore as the tide was coming in. Then he said to the rising tide: 'You are subject to me, as the land on which I am sitting is mine, and no one has resisted my overlordship with impunity. I command you, therefore, not to rise on to my land, nor to presume to wet the clothing or limbs of your master.'[23]

The set-up is beautifully put, as is what comes next, when he dead-pans: 'But the sea came up as usual and disrespectfully drenched the king's feet and shins.' It's the 'as usual' that bursts the balloon so perfectly – and that provoked a new humility in Cnut, who exclaimed, 'Let all the world know that ... there is no king save Him by whose will heaven, earth, and sea obey eternal laws.' Thereafter, Henry relates that his crown was never worn, but adorned instead an 'image of the crucified Lord'.

These narratives are rarely social histories; their purpose

is to assess each ruler by the same spiritual yardstick. In the twentieth century, Chesterton argued that politics still stumbled on the old eternal rocks – both conservatives and progressives preoccupied with immediate time rather than eternity, dooming them to endless revolution. From the midst of war, George Orwell (no admirer of the Catholic's relentless paradoxes) acknowledged that England's future could only be gained and reframed by some equivalent to the kingdom of heaven: 'We have got to be children of God', he pondered, 'even though the God of the Prayer Book no longer exists.'

This evening at Devil's Den, sat on the capstone, time is weightless. We are briefly, mercifully suspended.

Unutterable existence

It is eternity now. I am in the midst of it. It is about me in the sunshine.

Richard Jefferies[24]

The sky fumes, sarsen-grey. By the time I reach Richard Jefferies's monument, a stone stump just off the Ridge-way, I am drenched. Dressed as usual in jeans and old tweed jacket, these now slap and stick as I kick myself for resisting again waterproof walkers' gear. Oilskins, that's what I need.

Wherever the sun must be this morning, Jefferies's words still shine. Wiltshire's greatest nature writer (and more popular now than ever in his lifetime – abridged by tuberculosis at the age of thirty-eight), held a valiant, unorthodox faith that sought to shake off 'traditions acquired compulsorily' – all the relics of Christianity that he felt obstructed the clear, free reach of his soul. In his autobiographical work *The Story of My Heart*, he describes a moment 'of intense communion' in early adulthood, when, in a field on the Marlborough Downs, he lay in the grass and – ravished with the presence of it all – prayed (though 'prayer is a puny thing to it, and the word is a rude sign to the feeling') to and through the scene before him, 'that I might touch to the unutterable existence infinitely higher than deity'. His atheism – if it can be called that – was thus born from a longing for tran-scendence, and deeply spiritual.

To pray is to consider oneself addressed (in every sense – placed, engaged, spoken to) by life, and so honour that call with a response. However articulated, prayer is the soul's reply and begun not with our own launching faith, but a landing realization that we truly are here, and now – and the attendant hope we may be noticed. What Edward Thomas (writing about Jefferies) called nature's 'great flood of physical and spiritual sanity' grounds this apprehension, which is clearest felt when walking alone. Then it is we hear the earth resound our presence, like praise: the rubble and ruck of my boots as I tread, a couple of cows' heads turning aside as I pass, the flattened grass my testimony. There are days when nature is our advocate and we can let it speak for us.

Given Richard Jefferies's preference for long, unaccompanied walks, there is a certain enjoyable irony in his memorial being shared with a contemporary: Alfred Williams, 'the Hammerman poet', who laboured at the nearby Swindon railway works. They are, nevertheless, natural companions. Away from the deafening din of industry, Williams found release beyond words in these fields. 'Company in solitude' concludes the engraved tribute, inches from his neighbour: each of them silent in the face of glory.

> All my being is concentred in this little plot of ground;
> Here I live as one translated, careless in a world of toil,
> Pleased to wear the human fetter, journeying out along
>   the road
> With eternity around me, happy in my mortal soil,
> Climbing through the silent valley up the universe to
>   God.
>
> *Alfred Williams, 'About Wilts'*[25]

Even as the green herb

A tumble-dried July morning: damply warm and the lawn skipping with frogs. Reminded of Kipling's line about the 'toad beneath the harrow' (which I only know from Wodehouse, as Bertie Wooster's exclamation of his woes to an unmoved Jeeves), I nevertheless feel the need to mow – not only as our small meadow has grown its own Lockdown thatch, but also to find personal pasture.

For such a noisy task, I have always found mowing the grass an ideal aid to reflection. This is partly because doing so brings me close to my remembered father. The smell of four-star slugging into an old Mountfield, its snarling start-up (after several sweaty tugs on the recoil cord) and a gardening jacket itched with clippings: these things settle me, somehow.

Interviewing the then poet laureate Andrew Motion some years ago, I learned that he experienced the same powerful, filial connection. His 2010 volume *The Cinder Path* closes with its beautiful evocation in 'The Mower', in which he describes his recently departed dad 'trundling the Ransome out' for its ritual ignition:

> off came the brake and off charged the machine
> dragging you down to the blazing Tree of Heaven.[26]

The work is also both simple and manual enough to distract my usual preoccupations, thereby affording a little everyday reverie. The same is true, I found, when you use more traditional means of subduing the earth. In April, faced with a knee-high field – so close to the River Kennet it had remained waterlogged throughout our soggy winter – my son and I borrowed an antique scythe, our only option. Double-handed, with a twisted shaft and claw-ing two-and-a-half-foot blade, this tool is the means by which, over countless centuries, teams of mowers would rock themselves into cider-quenched oblivion.

Quite the most exhausting job, summoning long-dormant muscles (afterwards I splayed madly on the lawn like a parched blackbird), traditional mowing is also remarkably satisfying once you pick up the rhythm. This is found when the sound is right – a kind of rasping swathe, as when cows munch steadily past. Cathartic, too, if one brings to mind images from Scripture of cut grass and last judgement, which add a certain dramatic urgency to the mower's role.

Our years, we are reminded by Psalm 90, 'fade away suddenly like the grass. In the morning it is green and groweth up, but in the evening it is cut down, dried up and withered.' Alarmingly, this lease of life is pictured under the scythe of God's wrath, as a spur to our more profit-able labour. I have read these lines – with their evergreen hook, 'The days of our age are threescore years and ten' – at untold funerals, sparing mourners the more blade-like words, as a stake or bid on salvation by grace alone.

Death, wrote Belloc (in his flawless essay, 'The Mowing of a Field'), should be represented with a scythe and time with a sickle – for time is about the reaping of something ripe, while death 'comes always too soon', like hay is best cut just ahead of readiness. It's a bleak enough thought, but the monotonous swing of scything is described by Belloc as a kind of liturgy or mantra – its labour enabling the mower to rise above life's brevity:

> In this mowing should be like one's prayers – all of a sort and always the same, and so made that you can establish a monotony and work them, as it were, with half your mind: that happier half, the half that does not bother.

A rotary lawnmower requires far less art, of course – and more manhandling – but still allows me to hover away for an hour or so: hauled back, like a memory.

Elijah's cloud

The day being balmy, calm and free, we drove north-west to Malmesbury. Although still Wiltshire, it is just beyond my diocesan bounds, so today we were tourists – taking the route through Brinkworth, whose enjoyably large sign proclaims it as 'the longest village in England'. You wouldn't really know this (the settlement being so strung out) without its twin sign, over four miles later, astounding drivers from the other direction. It was, we agreed, an exceedingly long village.

Malmesbury itself is neither lengthy nor large, but the spectacular wreck of its abbey church amplifies the town's significance immeasurably. For this was one of Europe's principal seats of medieval scholarship, home to its second-greatest library and two of the nation's foremost chroniclers: St Aldhelm, who founded the abbey in the impossibly distant year of 676, and the Anglo-Norman monk William of Malmesbury, who illuminated the Dark Ages from a post-Conquest perspective. William's two major works, 'The Deeds of the Kings of the English' and 'The Deeds of the Bishops of England', are the source for most of what we know of Anglo-Saxon England after the death of Bede. The most concrete-set secularist would have to concede that, overwhelmingly, it was the clergy who invented English history. To bring the point home, even Athelstan, grandson of Alfred the Great and regarded as the first king of all England, found his rest among Malmesbury's persistent stones. Renowned for his piety and courage, Athelstan, entombed, has his eyes half-closed, with an almost-smile about his lips, as if mildly amused by paradise.

Aldhelm's monastery lasted for over eight centuries until dissolved by Henry VIII, though it was an electrical storm a few years before that brought the abbey to tumbling ruin and felled the spire that soared a precocious thirty feet higher than its rival at Salisbury. Constructed in lead-covered wood (not stone, like the latter), it stood on a tower of limestone, from where the great St Aldhelm's bell would be rung to drive away thunder. Yet a lightning strike could charge through all of this quicker than a nerve, convulsing the saturated walls. It must have felt like Jerusalem had fallen from heaven.

That Malmesbury Abbey remains a flourishing parish church, with flat whites at the café and services streamed on YouTube, is such a familiar miracle it fails to surprise us. For the same endurance is replicated in every community across Wiltshire and only now are we wondering whether, for some, time might finally be up. Returning home, my wife Rebecca remarks, wryly, that my photographs of church buildings tend not to include people.

She's right, and I wonder why – probably because, despite a lifetime spent in the houses of the Lord, only lately have I loved them. Something has changed since I began calling into so many when no one is there. In the long hours of their emptiness: this, paradoxically, is when they have come alive.

William of Malmesbury records Wulfstan, Bishop of Worcester, saying of his flock, 'We are ... neglecting souls and toiling at piling up stones.' Pulling into the drive, I meet a warden whose eight-hundred-year-old Grade I listed church, she says, has come to a crossroads. Four regular elderly attendees, five on the PCC, three resigning this year and £9,000 in annual costs to conjure from the collection plate.

She is my first such visitor, I say, but won't be the last: this potential closure is like Elijah's cloud, no bigger than a hand, which betokens an oncoming squall. Perhaps, too, the promise of renewal. The future of our historic church buildings is – like all they represent – a concern both national and local. It requires, or so I have thought, a more confidently strategic approach than we have hitherto taken. Of all people, we should surely be those who can face without fear the ending of things, knowing what Good Friday brings in its wake. Yet as it advances, the more pastoral the task becomes: and the more these stones start looking like sheep.

Raising Ebenezer

Wiltshire's reclining curves have human form: her furrowed brows an expression of social history. In the way one comes to know a familiar face, I am learning, slowly, to read these inscrutable hills: to understand their frowning contours.

Most such lines are made by walking: whether the rippling sheep-tracks or deeper, Iron Age lynchets formed by plough teams and plodding oxen. Each one is a measure of time and intention – even the feint flattening of hay that crossed my path this week on the downs: smooth and about a badger's width, leading, like a Richard Long sculpture, straight into a fence. Hilaire Belloc, in his 1911 odyssey *The Old Road*,[27] considers this creaturely progression as a key to appreciating the mystique of pathways:

> It was the most imperative and the first of our necessities. It is older than building and than wells; before we were quite men we knew it, for the animals still have it today; they seek their food and their drinking-places, and, as I believe, their assemblies, by known tracks which they have made.

Following these gives us a sense of life en route, poised (as St Augustine wrote) between memory and expectation: the present moment animated, motivated, by both the 'no-longer' and the 'not-yet'. Reflecting on Augustine and also Heidegger, especially the latter's conception of existence as a *project* – a sallying-forth, by which we are 'thrown ahead of ourselves into the future' – the philosopher William Barrett writes how:

the past is a field over which the searchlights of our vision continually play in order to extract different possibilities for our future; and consequently, the past is not external but internal to the present and also to the future, in the light of whose possibilities we are constantly restructuring the past.[28]

Because of this flow, we are prone to marking the march of time spatially, like Samuel in his back-and-forth forays against the Philistines. In both advance and retreat, Scripture places the word 'ebenezer' (literally 'stone of help') as a measurement of divine providence. After the victory that secured his possession of the Promised Land, 'Samuel took a stone and set it up between Mizpah and Jeshanah and named it Ebenezer, for he said, "Thus far the LORD has helped us."' 'Thus far' is the heart of Israel's covenantal view of history, which, as has often been remarked, bestowed on Western civilization its own sense of developing, meaningful timeline.

The present, as we experience it, is therefore both pushed and pulled forward, like a magnetic train. Prehistoric landscapes bring this home to us by so visibly containing the ancient past in the here and now. Recently, among the boulder streams of Fyfield Down – processions of sarsen left behind as the Ice Age receded – I found a fallen standing stone known as a *polissoir* or 'polisher': used as a bench for grinding axe heads in the Neolithic period. Sleek as marble, deeply lined and several thousand years older than the myth of Samuel, I can slide my hand into its fingers and sweep the dished surface, as if those working it have simply slipped out along the Ridgeway, to hunt or haunt the countryside.

Reading ahead

The dash is back, across Salisbury Plain. Claas combine harvesters section the fields into Minecraft blocks; static stacks of traffic form henges at roundabouts along the A303; delivery drivers dab their tablets and all is once more baled and busy.

My calendar, similarly, has been squared into life, the oblique weeks of Lockdown now a mosaic of meetings. This is why we tend only to follow the immediate outlook: keeping two chevrons apart to avoid collision. Such a timeframe feels truly secular, in the sense of being confined by the present period.

As one of its leaders, I am concerned that the national Church sees beyond the present, around the corner, in order to give confident guidance. A rank of bishops is always prone to appearing tank-like and monolithic, yet (as with our chessboard counterparts) we ought to move diagonally: to oversee the English Church, but – *pace* Emily Dickinson – oversee it slant. Recently, we have seemed peculiarly reactive and captive to the age: boxed in by successive crises.

The modern era mapped time and space like the New York streetscape, navigating chaos with an imposed grid: ideal for keeping your eyes in front, but blinding an episcopal view. Resisting the cul-de-sac of modernity, the Situationist movement of the 1950s and 1960s offered instead the *flâneur*, a strolling citizen who wandered off at a tangent, followed their nose and meandering desire lines, like a grazing creature. This allowed a new way of observing the urban scene, by wilful disobedience of the signs.

As a reminder of our social agency, this kind of liberty is vital (and why, incidentally, my children and I always swivel like Clangers when walking past a 'no turning' notice posted in an ample driveway). But while situationism was a disruptive stance, like all deconstructive gestures it lacked any meaningful direction. Jean-Francois Lyotard famously badged the postmodern attitude as 'incredulity towards metanarratives'.

To shepherd these times (not be tossed about by them, like a stone in a hub cap) we have to learn our way by heart – via the remembered landmarks that lead us home. So often our thinking about vision and strategy is entirely abstract, giving the illusion of progress, but as far from the ground as the satellites steering our vehicles. A bishop's oversight is of a particular place, and needs tracing as such.

What landscape historians call the 'mnemonic' knowledge of ancient routes is akin to the way we read a narrative text, which never looks at one passage alone, but takes in the lines before and after. Reading ahead – tacitly knowing the approaching words from the sense of those receding – requires, of course, a believable story about the future. The nation's current cultural dyslexia turns the present into a perpetual series of barriers – trip hazards, to be clambered over or avoided. The Church knows of an alternative route, if we can but recall it.

Awful monitor

A breath of vestry prayer, then up with the mask and in we process. My last visit to St John's, Devizes was in March: the annual Service for the Rule of Law, called by the High Sheriff. Traditionally responsible to the monarch for maintenance of law and order in each county, the Sheriff ('shire-reeve') is the country's oldest secular office after the Crown, and among its incumbents' historic duties they provided the judiciary with a retinue of javelin men to defend them on their journeys to court. The Wiltshire judges' short circuit to church (after robing at the Town Hall, amid wig tins and bonhomie) was this year fraught with no more than a little local incredulity – was this a re-enactment of some kind? – and some nascent concerns about social distance, as their pillar of clouded heads filed into St John's, flocking the pews.

On that occasion – afar remote after our four-month gulf – I preached from St Paul's incomparable reflection on the inner conflict: 'I agree that the law is good ... but sin ... dwells within me ... I can will what is right, but I cannot do it.' Reviewing my script, I see myself suggesting that the coming pandemic would test which of our inbuilt tendencies might rise to the surface, rehearsing the ancient, biblical see-saw between legalism and grace, and observing how the Christian framing of our common law was original to the nation itself. This kind of remark (which I feel increasingly called to make) is almost bound to sound reactionary, not radical – a geriatric institution shaking a stick at its secular grandchildren. Yet the deeper one digs, the more one discovers the Church at the roots of things – which rightly brings guilt along with responsibility. We are up to our necks in this patch of soil.

Shortly before he died in 2004, the medieval historian Patrick Wormald, author of the magisterial *The Making of English Law*, gave a lecture in Canterbury, in which he considered the seventh-century legal code of King Aelthelbert of Kent – 'the first surviving text of any type written by as well as for Englishmen'. In this, he notes the pivotal importance of Christian conversion (Augustine having washed up on the Isle of Thanet some twenty years previously) in bringing vernacular literacy. While Latin or French superseded the old language, it will, he attests, have survived locally under the sheriff, before, in the fourteenth century, 'staging a remarkable "come-back", first as the literature of Chaucer, and before long as law made by Council and Parliament'. There is, he concludes, an indirect bond 'between the fact that England is today the world's oldest functioning state and that English is its most widely spoken language ... the history of both begins with Aethelbert'.[29]

While his law-code itself is a curiosity, mainly concerned with forensic attention to bodily harm ('he who smashes a chinbone is to pay up with 20 shillings'), it is the first example of this newly baptized people setting down what had previously been committed to memory – the legal implications of neighbourhood. If the codifying of English law was the earliest consequence of church-led literacy, its moral infiltration was perhaps the next, expressed nearly three centuries later in the laws of Alfred the Great. These are prefaced with tracts of Old Testament teaching – the monarch explaining how Mosaic law applied to Christian nations. Alfred writes:

> Afterwards, when it came about that many peoples had received the faith of Christ, many synods of holy bishops and also of other distinguished councillors were assembled ... throughout all the English people. They then established, through that mercy which Christ taught, that for almost every misdeed at the first offence secular lords might with their permission receive without sin the monetary compensation ...[30]

He adds: 'Then I, King Alfred, gathered them together and ordered to be written many of the ones that our forefathers observed', including Aethelbert of Kent – 'who first among the English people received baptism'.

What counts as mercy in one age will, of course, appear irredeemably harsh in another. Yet for a faith with human frailty at its origin – and saving grace as its heart – I never fail to be astonished how readily believers have arrogated the judgement of God. Exiting the west door of St John's, someone from the congregation indicates to me a striking, fifteen-foot-high obelisk in the graveyard – 'our monument to misspent youth'. One side describes 'the sudden and awful end' of five young people drowned in a nearby pond, one Sunday evening in 1751. On another is inscribed the fourth commandment, 'as an awful monitor to young people to remember their creator in the days of their youth'. Whatever might compensate for such grief, it isn't this.

Whited sepulchres

The sins of England are written on our chancel walls, marbled and memorialized. At St Peter's Dorchester – like most parish churches, a crowding gallery of monuments – I am standing beneath one large but fairly inconspicuous plaque to John Gordon, a plantation owner who died here in 1774, aged forty-six. Masking-taped beneath this information is a temporary panel of cardboard explaining that 'The remainder of this memorial has been covered as it commemorates actions and uses language that are totally unacceptable to us today'. When revealed, the inscription goes on to describe how Gordon 'was signally instrumental in quelling a dangerous rebellion' in Jamaica – among slaves who 'finally yielded to their confidence in his humanity'. What that action indicated about Gordon's confidence in theirs is left unwritten.

It is an extraordinary epitaph, under which parishioners have murmured their prayers for two and a half centuries. The Parochial Church Council has periodically considered how best to address this affront, until lately the memorial has become an understandable focus for regional concern and media interest after being highlighted by Topple the Racists, the campaigning group that emerged from the actions of Bristolians in forcibly removing the statue of the slaver Edward Colston. There can be a blazing grace in protest, enabling us to see what we have been blind to for too long.

St Peter's has responded with exemplary good sense, researching the history of the Jamaican revolt thus recorded and drawing on pre-existing good relations with West Dorset Multicultural Network and the County Museum. Conveniently situated next door, the latter will in due course be receiving the Gordon plaque for permanent display, not least because of its singular potential for demonstrating how enslaved people were agents of their own freedom, not simply 'given' this by enlightened campaigners.

In the questionable way we allow cultural figures post-humously to colonize the landscape, this is Thomas Hardy Country. Indeed, a youthful Hardy was assistant architect for the refurbishment of St Peter's (as another sign here indicates), and that conjuror of lost Edens is himself memorialized in stone at nearby Stinsford churchyard, where pamphlets from the Thomas Hardy Society mingle with pew sheets on the welcome desk. In her insightful study, *Dorset's Hidden Histories*,[31] Louisa Adjoa Parker observes that Dorset has singular potency as an icon of England and so might seem an unlikely county in which to consider black history. If, however, Englishness is to be conceived more inclusively than hitherto, then it is the very place to address this: not simply to step over the artificial demarcation of minority ethnic communities as 'urban', but because the countryside is where love of the land is owned, unabashed. And unless all in that land have a route into loving it, alienation is the inevitable end.

The Church of England, being so entombed in our country's past, has a unique custodial role to play in curating such contested heritage – as its recent and welcome advice on the theme acknowledges – and in cultivating a patriotism that, as the proximate outworking of our love for the world, acknowledges the global reach of every local affection. By virtue of what Anglicans believe about eternity (that it has a more powerful magnetism than time), and about redemption (that we are not captive to past transgressions), they have at their disposal a singularly useful set of conceptual tools.

In particular, these imply that the rural past does not need to be quite so sacred, so unimpeachable. However unlikely it may sound, the problem of Britain's heritage is an eschatological one, for we remain enchanted by a vanished kingdom, not the coming one. The village church is rightly perceived as hallowing each plot, but rarely because of (or in preparation for) what lies ahead. Consecration, furthermore, is no kind of indulgence – not exemption from scrutiny – but the sacrifice of torn and imperfect things to God, in whose hands those fragments may be restored. Loving the land is a pastoral cure.

The trouble is that idylls are so easily idolized. Yet the admission of 'hidden histories' into the national story allows for a loyalty that may be balanced (rather than cancelled out) by the record of our wrongs, to which the countryside often bears a kind of protected witness. In her recent and provocative study, *Green Unpleasant Land*,

Corinne Fowler unpicks some of that tapestry, noting how rural England has ever been 'a terrain of inequalities', with many of its Arcadian treasures afforded through monumental folly and injustice. This does not mean they are not also transportingly beautiful and worthy of conservation, but does suggest that our approach to national remembrance should be more akin to the kind we encourage when reviewing our personal past – a blend, in other words, of justifiable pride, aching regret and, in maturity (one trusts), understanding and acceptance of the whole. Above all, as a nation we should love others as we love ourselves.

Just behind St Peter's in Dorchester is the prison, recently closed, where Robert Wedderburn – activist, Unitarian minister and the most prolific black writer in Britain at the start of the nineteenth century – was jailed for two years on a charge of seditious blasphemy. His supposed heresies included a description of Jesus Christ as 'a genuine radical reformer'. Wedderburn was visited here by William Wilberforce and upon release composed his work *The Horrors of Slavery*,[32] informed by early experiences in Jamaica.

Each generation is at liberty to interrogate those who came before (especially those with power and control), bringing them to a time of trial. The tougher existential question is what sentencing power to give the current one, which again concerns the ultimate ends of things. In the Christian schema, earth's last judgement was passed, once and for all, in the events surrounding Jesus Christ – especially those of his Passion and resurrection. The historic gospel is thus also our Domesday Book, and for this reason Christians ought not capitulate to the annihilating myth of an ultimate or absolute present – but, rather, one that is entirely contingent upon both past and future, and whose claims are responsible to both.

Racial justice, like all other kinds, is demanded by our common destiny – that is, a new humanity, wrought

(Christians believe) at the cross. This does not downplay the 'urgency of now' – as the Church of England's report *From Lament to Action*[33] frames the case – but means that justice is never captive to the present. Instead it summons us like a voice through fog, drawing us on to see its emerging visage. That the appearance of righteousness has altered so strikingly through time – and will do so again – urges humility in all pronouncements upon our forebears, in light of our own eventual reckoning.

Dorchester's street map forms a fallen stick man. It being a glorious afternoon, I explore further up the vertebrae of London Road to conclude my visit with a swift circuit of Poundbury, The Prince of Wales' extravagant essay on the built environment. A screen of sunlight and serene sky enhances the impression of this suburb as a kind of simulacrum – a faux-accidental collision of Victorian terrace, Georgian parade and rustic cosiness. Impossibly pristine, Poundbury is a full-scale mock-up, flanked by site hoardings and poised JCBs, ready to confect more samples from the pattern book of English archetypes. It should be scandalous to like it, but I do – and suspect I could all too easily keep up the pretence.

There is no parish church, tellingly – the one essential component of the rural scene that could not be admitted. A pity, as this could orientate the place a little, even offer a truer perspective on our heritage. And where this has been weighed in the balance and found wanting.

Preserved in Imber

Imber isn't easy to see. Camouflaged like a curlew, the stone tower of St Giles' Church emerges about half a mile from the village, as you approach from the south. This is about as deep into Salisbury Plain as it is possible to be: 'Little Imber on the down; seven miles from any town', ran the local rhyme, before civilian access to the village was blocked by the Ministry of Defence during World War Two. Like its better-known counterpart in Dorset, Tyneham, Imber was evacuated in 1943 to provide a training area for US troops preparing for the allied invasion of Europe. A lane leading into the village, 'American Road', is one reminder of their residency, as are the railway tracks strengthening the curbs against Sherman tanks in nearby Shrewton.

Imber is now open to the public for twenty days a year, during which the well-preserved parish church receives nigh on fifteen thousand visitors. Hearing this, I'm momentarily tempted to call for the evacuation and closure of all Wiltshire's parishes, in order to spark their nostalgic revival. Next Saturday, scores more will rumble down the Imber Road from Warminster in (what else?) specially chartered Routemaster buses. But what draws them? Surely the myth of settlement and the irresistible thrill of decline: black-eyed homes, overgrown greenery and the uncanny thought that, when every other village is lit, Imber will remain dark.

Yet whatever kind of place Imber is today – part stage set for army manoeuvres (ironically, these husks of houses are used for urban operations training), part pop-up museum or pilgrimage site – it is hardly a lost Eden and by no means abandoned. During the 2000s, I learn, several hundred Afghans were brought here in order to recreate an authentic bustling bazaar, around which troops patrolled, observed from above by incredulous buzzards.

Nature reigns in Imber and comes uncommonly close: roe deer lope over the road, a red kite takes flight, mere feet away, and the encircling fields jitter with butterflies. My guide, a conservation volunteer with a privileged red pass to visit these restricted areas, has spent twenty years mapping and logging them – butterflies, ponds (all 290 of them) and the winterbournes that vein this pulsing land-scape. The detailed attention of such latter-day Gilbert Whites means that Salisbury Plain, while barely inhabited, remains deeply, devoutly known.

Ghosted by plastic sheeting, the altar in St Giles' awaits the next service (like the buses, there are two or three a year) – a baptism, remarkably, although the incumbent informs me he will need to bring a salad bowl, the font having long since departed. Quite regularly, I come across furnishings from Imber that were scattered across the diocese when the future of the church was in question.

Happily, the Churches Conservation Trust now cares for the building, which is already realizing its singular potential as an emblem of persistent Anglican faith.

We aren't to stray beyond the road: military debris is everywhere strewn in this mock battlefield. Passing carcasses of never-inhabited homes erected in the 1970s for training, it can appear that everything here is a facade – with an emotional force that is highly charged but, ultimately, blank. Then you realize Imber was dwelt in for 900 years, making its zero return in the national census (shown continually since 1951) deeply poignant – pregnant even. As we leave, a lone volunteer tugs the bells of St Giles into life. For us? Maybe, but as they ring across the unharvested fields, it feels as though the land could be rising to worship.

Mawddach

Holidays hallow the whole year, hold a sacred place in our past. In almost every grief-stilled living room I have entered – notebook and teacup poised, like the mood, between spillage and restraint – it is to holidays the bereaved return: as if these were the weeks that mattered. The caravan in Morecambe, that place in the Lakes, the crammed car, Dad more relaxed. This homing in isn't disproportionate – we know full well the other fifty weeks of the year are where ordinary life occurred – it is simply our need for sabbath: for certain seasons to be festive and different, to renew the balance and make sense of the rest.

As a child, fascinated by the succession of dates on the spines of my annuals, on my father's *Parson's Pocketbook* diaries, summer holidays formed a chain of memory, a way of telling the time. I took pride in being able to reel off the years and the locations, straining to focus the earliest, blurry recollections. The older, the better. Most powerful of all in personal myth-making are destinations we revisit, whose simplest features (which would soon be dulled if we were to remain there) become totems of wonderful recognition – the café is still there! – extending our infant delight in repeated play, in disappearance and return.

Once laid down, these dormant impressions can be awoken in a moment. So it only takes a waft of wet bracken and I am back in North Wales, on another reluctant walk: Snowdonia, through a Thermos-fogged windscreen. This August, at short notice, we were invited to Bodowen, a house in Barmouth where we have stayed, every couple of summers, for fifteen years. Formerly the home of the Himalayan adventurer Bill Tillman (lost at sea in his eightieth year, piloting a tug towards the Falklands – the glowing ashes of his image, dauntless behind moustache and pipe, still greet visitors aboard), Bodowen affords an unrivalled panorama of the Mawddach estuary, as it yawns into Cardigan Bay.

Mostly we've driven here late at night, often after Evensong on a Sunday, descending through a notch in the crags above Dolgellau, to peel sleeping children from their seats and arise to a landscape that places all else in the background. Slate hills, purpled with heather; the viaduct's delicate neckline; Cadair Idris, climbing through theophanic mist. Our friends are selling up, so this will be our last time in this God-haunted spot, particularly poignant for teenagers anticipating their own, opening horizon. There is, consequently, a heightened desire to rekindle former joys – from car soundtrack ('Glory Bound' by The Wailin' Jennys, Ben Folds's 'Jesusland') to day trips (Harlech, for junk shops and fabric, Tan-y-Bwlch station on the Ffestiniogg Railway, for the enveloping sweetness of steam from a footbridge).

Just before Harlech Castle's formidable silhouette crowns the headland, we pull off to find the church of St Tanwg, buried in the dunes like a snoozing granddad or abandoned dinghy. An unpromising prism to begin with, its plain medieval shell houses possibly the oldest Christian foundation in the country, presumed to date from St Patrick's Irish mission in the AD 430s. Inside, prone or prostrate by the altar, is the Ingenuus Stone, a striking fifth-century pillar, inscribed 'Ingenui' with its owner's name and carried, so it is thought, from the Wicklow Hills of Ireland. Until the 1960s, with common-sense utility, it was employed as a lintel over the church door. Tanwg is associated with this church only, and holy days stretching back over the sand.

Petrifying well

Midday at the Petrifying Well in Knaresborough, North Yorkshire. Strings of small teddies hang like mountaineers from the sheer face, sops of fur hardening by degrees; a plastic lobster with calcified claws; a toy rabbit, dangling by its ears. Scores of us watch this dripping gibbet, transfixed by its surreal assortment of common or cuddly things slowly turning to stone. An unspecific bulge on the rippling slab above us is, we are informed, a Victorian top hat, left there in 1853.

Mother Shipton's Cave, billed as 'Britain's oldest tourist attraction', has drawn paying customers since 1630 to witness this curious alchemy, caused by the unusually high mineral content in the springs cascading into the River Nidd. 'Mother' Ursula Shipton herself was a renowned soothsayer in Tudor England, born and raised in near-prehistoric conditions in the wedged-shaped cave a few yards from the well, her bent figure and portentous maxims becoming an archetype for pub signs and side-show crones. Having predicted 'triumphant death will ride London through', she is cited by Samuel Pepys after the Great Fire, the diarist commenting 'Mother Shipton's word is out'.

While some of her prognostications seem prescient enough ('iron in the water shall float as easy as a wooden boat', 'carriages without horses shall go'), the real wonder may be how poor Ursula survived such isolation and penury into old age. Winter in this cave would turn most of us to stone, one way or another. The money that continues to be made here (£45 will buy you a dejected-looking bear that looks as if it has fallen into a concrete mixer) is testament to our endless fascination for animate life becoming frozen, somehow – whether Lot's wife, turned into a pillar of salt for glancing back at Sodom, or C. S. Lewis's chilling sculpture park of cursed creatures – to my mind, the most memorable scene in Narnia.

Before we, too, begin to fossilize, I'm keen to fit in two other nearby sites on this short tour – a reunion with family after the estrangement of recent months – stopping first at three standing stones known as The Devil's Arrows. Retreating, like Lot, from a bright new housing development ('Escape to a home that's the right size for you' urges a noticeboard), my leaflet observes that the highest of these standing stones, at 22 feet 6 inches, is 'taller than anything at Stonehenge'. Wiltshire pride duly chastened, we trace the line of these extraordinary shafts, which sharpen slightly at the top and have been weathered into digits resembling enormous, petrified paws.

It was a radiant evening, honey-toned, with conversation melting freely as we ambled back to the car through the cornfield. Going with the flow, we chose to drive on to Myton: site of one of the most curious battles in English history. In the early fourteenth century, Yorkshire was a vulnerable place on the political map, prone to cross-border raids following the Battle of Bannockburn in 1314. Edward I – 'The Hammer of the Scots' – having stepped in to arbitrate disputes over succession to the Scottish throne, proceeded violently to assert his own claim as 'Lord Paramount', bludgeoning this home by the removal to Westminster Abbey of the Stone of Destiny, used for centuries in Scottish coronation ceremonies. Slung like a hassock under King Edward's Chair, this discomfiting cushion (also known as Jacob's Pillow, or the Stone of Scone) has bolstered national coronations ever since. The significance of its return to Scotland, on St Andrew's Day 1996, can hardly be overestimated.

Bannockburn confirmed Scotland's resurgence against Edward's hapless son, Edward II. In 1318, while the king was occupied trying to recapture Berwick, Scottish forces pushed south, hoping to entrap the English Queen, then in residence at York. It was left to William Melton, the Archbishop of York, to muster a force comprised, incredibly, of substantial numbers of clergy, secular and religious. Quite how the 'Chapter of Myton' (as this bizarre army became known) expected to repel such an attack is almost comical to envisage, but, drawn to a field between two rivers at Myton-on-Swale and with the Scots blocking their escape, they were purely lambs unto the shambles. Scores of monks attempted to flee across the river where, weighed down by woollen habits, they were either drowned or slaughtered.

Standing in the dusk on the bridge above this carnage – distanced by time, though not by space – there's little need for fortune-telling. The ground itself can prophesy.

Hercules Buildings

'Everybody does not see alike', writes William Blake. 'The tree which moves some to tears of joy is in the eyes of others only a green thing that stands in the way.'[34] Blake's blood was up: he was responding in a letter to a Reverend Dr Trusler, of Hercules Buildings, Lambeth, who had commissioned artwork from his neighbour, but found it too fanciful. A stick thrust into the swirling hive of his imagination, Blake's riposte fizzes with stinging insight. 'Why is the Bible more entertaining and instructive than any other book?' he presses: 'Is it not because [it is] addressed to the imagination, which is spiritual sensation?'

That the imagination is our highest faculty for apprehending truth was an article of faith for the Romantic movement, and one with deeply theological implications – as Samuel Taylor Coleridge, in particular, was later to expound. Modern thought had increasingly grounded metaphysical flights, deifying the rational mind: Coleridge had different ideas. Indeed, for him the biblical portrayal of God as Trinity was 'the idea of ideas', from which all others proceeded. Human reason was not supreme, but a reflection – an emanation – of the divine mind and character. Convalescing from opium addiction in nearby Calne (from which his existential reflections in the *Biographia* emerged), the poet concluded, 'We see all things in God.'

Dismissing believers as those with 'an imaginary friend' is a commonplace taunt but one worth embracing, I think. For the plain truth is that God, not being visible, must be imagined – and it is surprising, therefore, that our sermons give so little space for considering the central place of imagination in realizing faith. All of our friends – on earth or above – are, in part at least, imaginary: we cannot conceive them otherwise. The question is how much of what we imagine is true, and what is fanciful as fairies on a foxglove.

Our ideas are trialled by experience: will their bright wings bear our weight? Equally, by where they transport us, or the world they construct. Coleridge separates our basic (or 'primary') imagination – the everyday picture of life we frame – and highlights the 'secondary imagination' as the creative ability to reassemble this collage of images into something new and meaningful. But the matter is the same: whatever we see – whether in a tree, train or trombone – is filtered, tinted and retouched by each person's perception.

Many have found in this impulse to recreate an echo or expression of the divine image in humanity. Indeed, the premise of Scripture is that we are God's idea before he is ours: hatched from his matchless imaginings, sparked into life. Our six-day labours to make something of what has been given us thus begin in the heart and mind. The talentless slave in Christ's parable fails not by his actions primarily, but in how he imagines the master. 'As a man is', remarks Blake to Dr Trusler, 'so he sees.'

*Consider it all
for show —
not rooted in
Incarnation*

Vectis

In the model village at Godshill, Isle of Wight, a christening. Parents and elderly parson assemble outside, while an invisible congregation sings (for some reason) 'Abide With Me' – pointed to the skies, where the life-sized All Saints looms above, massive in comparison. Setting aside images from the final scenes of *Hot Fuzz* – which take place in a similar setting and with an eye-watering denouement involving the church spire – we count four such Russian-dolled reproductions, the smallest an approximate blotch with a tower like a stock cube.

This place is all about a sense of scale, if not proportion: our fascination for creating miniature versions of reality that are, inevitably, somewhat slower to change than their animated originals. In his sparkling 1998 satire *England, England*,[35] Julian Barnes imagined the entire Isle of Wight becoming annexed and developed as a theme park of archetypal Englishness – Robin Hood, Stonehenge, Anne Hathaway's Cottage – a project that founders, hilariously, on the hubris and chaos of human behaviour when extracted from its natural habitat. Christian heritage haunts the novel: towards the end, its central character, Martha Cochrane, finds herself in an abandoned medieval church on the island, pondering the faith of those buried nearby and her own, growing desire for authenticity. Having rejected as a lie the imposed Christianity of her childhood, she nevertheless feels a sense of cultural bereavement – 'a discontent with the thinness of life' – reflecting:

An individual's loss of faith and a nation's loss of faith, aren't they much the same? Look what happened to England. Old England. It stopped believing in things. Oh, it still muddled along. It did OK. But it lost seriousness.

The problem, she considers, is that the vocabulary of Christian belief no longer answers that continuing need: 'the words don't seem to fit the thoughts nowadays.' Words – and their meaningful translation – have been the basic missionary challenge for the Church since its inception, however acutely this has been felt during Christendom's long recession. When its words no longer fit the culture, the Church generally faces two temptations: to settle in an artificial past when they did, or create an alternative present where they do.

Both nostalgia and sectarianism are a manipulation – an imaginative denial – of time and space: creating worlds within a world, microcosms of how life might or ought to be. All groups do this to some degree, in order to foster community and shared values – and how we need them! Growing up, I found in evangelical subculture a refuge, somewhere to belong – offering as it did a kind of nursery garden for young believers. The test of authenticity, of maturity, is how these relate to life outside the model village: how, in other words, we love a world unlike our own. As with nations, the Church runs into danger when it becomes an island entire unto itself, growing an exaggerated, aberrant view of its own ideal and unassailable home.

Plump as a row of hassocks, the cottages leading up to All Saints, Godshill form (Pevsner comments) 'one of the Isle of Wight's picture postcard motifs', noting that 'the village has become a show village and not without reason'. Such appealing thatchiness presents a challenge, suggesting that the parish is some sort of replica. Yet on the wall of the church's south chapel is painted a unique and mysterious depiction of Jesus: crucified on a flourishing three-boughed plant, thought to be a lily. 'The lily cross', dating from the mid-fifteenth century and discovered in 1835, finds Christ slimly suspended in the tangle of nature, as though he were another wayward limb.

It seems probable that this commemorates the rare calendrical occurrence when Good Friday coincides with the Feast of the Annunciation (the lily being a symbol of the Virgin Mary) – abridging the incarnation in a single day. One old rhyme runs:

When the Lord's Day falls in Our Lady's lap, England shall meet with a great mishap.

While it may be past, this intertwining of our nation's fate and faith was not some conceit, but a genuine thing – and if the Church, in age, is to bud again, it must be rooted in the same, nameable spot.

Acts of enclosure

Parsnips, carrots and beans are carved into the memorial stone for Gerrard Winstanley, which stands aloof from the circuiting traffic: a radical spade jammed into private soil. As notices at every entrance remind you, the 964 gated acres of St George's Hill are emphatically not common ground, even if, for a few weeks in 1649, they were proclaimed as such, when Winstanley and his small band of Diggers broke the earth as a prophetic sign of the coming, kingless kingdom.

I last explored this part of Surrey in the late 1970s, when my uncle, who lived in Byfleet, led us to trespass on to the disused remains of the Brooklands motor racing track. Scrambling up a wooded verge, we emerged to see a vast curve of silent tarmac, scattered with brambles and banking giddily towards its sudden truncation. This was the undismantled past – a glitch of history – and its impact has remained with me since.

Today, though, I was searching for the roots of an idea – the radical patriotism of the English Revolution. For anyone trying to reconceive in our own day the Church's national role, the Interregnum following the death of Charles I is a uniquely fertile field – being the only time when the uninterrupted course of Church and state (with its divine underwriting of monarchy and problematic links with landed power) was abruptly halted.

In this hothouse of ideologies, Gerrard Winstanley flourished briefly, though fruitfully: setting a few dozen friends 'to plant and manure the wasteland' on St George's Hill and pamphleting this tiny rebellion 'to all the powers of the world' as a reclamation of the earth from those who, for centuries, had held it in bondage as private property. Writing in a manual, vernacular style that sparked like a shovel on flint, his intention was the peaceful overthrow of those encroaching acts of enclosure that were already transforming the national landscape and economy. Strikingly, Winstanley's polemic is soaked in scriptural analogy, his indignation at the tyranny of landlords entirely grounded in the Word of God, which bisected England and found it maggoty at the core:

> I tell thee, thou England, thy battles now are all spiritual, dragon against the Lamb, and the power of love against the power of covetousness.[36]

This ferocious apocalyptic was directed as much at the state Church (which had in Winstanley's lifetime reached the apogee of its worldly power under William Laud) as at the landed gentry. For Winstanley, hedges and church walls were all of a piece, indicating the sinful desire to control what ought to be a common treasury. The pursuit of property brought about a fall in man, infecting religious practice wherever it tried to annex the truth. In one of his most compelling tracts, addressed to 'all the several societies of people called churches', he attacks a tendency that is perhaps just as damaging today:

> For all your particular churches are like the enclosures of land which hedges in some to be the heirs of life, and hedges out others. But ... you shall find that Christ who is the universal power of love is not confined to parties or private chambers; but he is the power of life, light and truth now rising up to fill the earth with himself.

A few weeks after visiting St George's Hill – where Winstanley's vegetables adorn his monument like a mock coat of arms – I attended a seminar on land reform at Winchester University's Centre for English Identity and

Politics. Some 1 per cent of the population, we learned, owns half the territory, of which only 10 per cent is open access. It has long been an uneasy trope of national life that, as Defoe wrote, 'no one has any right to live in England but those to whom England belongs'. But when householders own just 5 per cent of the country and the Church Commissioners retain a 105,000-acre property portfolio, the world may need turning upside down once more – if only for the lesson that possession of the land can lead, unless we're careful, to the forfeit of our soul.

Post attendee

A quilt of mist embeds the Pewsey Vale this morning, punctured only by the pencil point of Bishop's Cannings church. Autumn's new routine is haring to Devizes with my eldest daughter, to drop her at the Pelican Inn for catching the bus to art college in Trowbridge. Along the A4 is such a sketchable landscape: I'm continually darting glances either side, longing to park and take some photos, before it all evaporates.

Grace is telling me about a friend who has moved away this week, keen to leave Marlborough behind. Given our affection for this new home, such antipathy is a reminder of how all places are a matter of perception: the town 'in itself' inseparable from the town as we perceive it. The High Street's broad trough, say, from the coffee queue at Greggs. With our particular perspective, we not only view the world differently but also, crucially, remake it in our image.

The larger the locale, the more invented it must become – by being harder to see and necessarily more idealized as the scope increases. We are bound always to be in several places at once, therefore, acting locally yet tacitly as part of other, more conceptual communities. Citizenship involves this kind of layered identification, in which all states are states of mind. Thus, we will be British, or European, or even 'global' when these badges symbolize something we love in common – or offer a perceived check on what we deplore. When such associations become alienating or objectionable we will think up alternatives, because place is, before anything else, an index of personal attachment. If we want to be at home in the world, we need first to be at home to ourselves.

Given that I am spending most of the week attending an online conference to clarify a national vision for the Church of England, these questions of scale are of immediate relevance, not least in suggesting where to start with such a task. On any map we need an arrow indicating 'You are here', which appears also to be the methodology of Scripture, in its central affirmation that the way God loved the world was by first loving it personally and locally. In Gospel stories the kingdom of heaven grows, as all life must, from particular to universal – being likened to various small things (seeds, yeast, pearls) that have value or potential well beyond their size. For the authors of the New Testament, the incarnation becomes a kind of fractal for the cosmos. In Christ, they claim, God takes place: and they write as though the splintered fingers of Jesus hold all things together.

This idea is by no means incidental to England's own self-understanding. Indeed, the doctrine of election, which held that divine purpose in choosing one person, or nation, must ever be the blessing of all, was a basic ingredient of emergent patriotism from the Elizabethan era onwards (and was still infusing the columns of popular historians like Arthur Bryant four centuries later). A pivotal question for Tudor polity was whether England was 'the' elect nation or just one among many. English exceptionalism, the source of so much arrogant damage at home and abroad, was heresy before it was hubris – namely, a denial of Pentecost, whereby each people (according to the book of Acts) received their own spiritual vocation, as myriad lands of hope and glory.

Nationalism, by definition, gives exaggerated priority to the nation and, fearing a hostile world, insists that all lesser local loyalties submit. Patriotism at its best arrows outward, not in: beginning with love of neighbour and imagining one's motherland from there. As Edmund Burke put it, local affection is the 'first link in the series by which we proceed towards a love to our country and to mankind'.

If the aim is universal, then loving Reading or Redcar will simply be a proximate means of loving the world.

And while Burke's 'little platoons' are rightly being reclaimed by present-day communitarians, it is to Coleridge that Anglicans could turn for a more virtuous vision of the national Church, informed as it was by a deep theological imagination. Coleridge's patriotism, like that of William Temple in the next century, was principally concerned with the cultivation of society and moral character. Although his conclusions sound strikingly similar to Burke's ('Jesus knew our nature – and that expands like the circles of a lake – the love of friends, parents and neighbours leads us to a love of our country to the love of all mankind'), he homes in explicitly on the role of the parish as a small parable of the kingdom – a 'germ of civilization, round which the capabilities of the place may crystallize and brighten'.

In practice, of course, parochialism has all too often been a constraining and insular thing – liable for raising 'oppression's humble slave', as John Clare scathingly begins his poetic satire, *The Parish*, written within a year or two of Coleridge's idealistic *On the Constitution of the Church and State*, yet painting an altogether different landscape. And while modern Britain is more unrecognizable yet, it is perhaps because we don't forget such complicity that most bishops remain ambivalent at best about our vestigial status as the established Church.

Zoom conference concluded and gleefully 'Post Attendee' once more, I'm able to drive out for a pastoral visit. Beyond Devizes, I stop to take in the parish church of St Mary the Virgin, Steeple Ashton: a soaring magnificat in stone. Above the door (and the earliest dated graffiti I've ever seen – '1579' etched in careful serifs) is a framed text – at a guess, from the eighteenth century. Quoting Proverbs 24.21, it reads, with leaden emphasis:

Fear thou the Lord and the King:
and meddle not
with them that are given to CHANGE.

It may be that the Church of England could better serve the
nation when finally unfastened from it. After all, Magna
Carta married the monarch's 'wish and command that the
English Church shall be free' to the liberties of its people,
'in all places and for ever'. Personally, I think and hope
not. But whether this comes to pass will, almost certainly,
depend less on the Church's vision for our nation than on
the country's perception of their Church.

Society of aliens

Bewildered locals pluck out their earbuds, interrupted for a moment. In what appears to be a scene from Trumptonshire, the town crier is booming out the news. Between spirited shakes of his handbell, we learn that 900 circuits of Wimborne Minster are about to begin – all 102 miles being paced out by one person, to raise funds in commemoration of the church's ninth centenary.

The Minster is a treasury of curios, including a dazzling fourteenth-century astronomical clock, whose pre-Copernican sun whirs around a turquoise earth. Outside, amid the oyezing, stand the mayor, the rector and myself, arrayed for the press: none of us (it must be emphasized) is dressed normally. Those not wearing a tricorn hat stay at a safe distance, while we join the first couple of laps like pace cars before peeling off as our companion continues alone. His shoes, he reassures me, have memory foam insoles.

These civic occasions, when the distinctive voices of Church and state still blend and blur are more than a glorified pantomime. We are performing, and thereby reinforcing, certain ideals of community, in which outlandish ritual and approximations of period costume play their part – or, rather, display that *we* are playing our part as stewards of an ancient legacy that both preceded and will, we trust, long outlive us. Such chains of memory are especially worth sustaining in this intense present, when even the recent cultural past feels out of reach. Chigley and Camberwick Green, those animated market towns of my infancy, with their McCartneyesque cast of sergeant-majors and firemen, are another country indeed.

The two cities, of God and humanity, 'are mingled together from the beginning to the end of our history', writes Augustine of Hippo in *De Civitate Dei* – and there is a tension, yet also a harmony between them. The ends of earthly civic life are to the more proximate goods of commonwealth, health and repose, which the heavenly citizen must order towards their eternal goal – 'peace, in life everlasting'. The heavenly city thus relates peace on earth to peace in the next world – which, of course, must be believed to be seen. This familiar (within Christian doctrine, at least) schema has the curious effect of subordinating the life we know and love to an imagined future – a world intangible. It is the kingdom of heaven that believers must seek first, before all other things.

To onlookers, this priority of the invisible can be puzzling, to say the least, for it appears to cheapen the very things that are most real and desirable to us. But perhaps the strangeness of the Christian world view is made more familiar when reckoning how imagined communities, past or present, are the very engine of human society: powering our purchases, shaping our desires, mobilizing our migration. Every one of us seeks an ideal home, and the roomier our heavenly dwellings, the better for those without them below.

In Augustine's paradigm – one of the load-bearing foundations of Western culture and famously framed by the disintegration of the Roman Empire – what remains obscure is the possibility of our present life touching upon the goods of heaven. Civic participation appears merely instrumental – as a 'society of aliens' the faithful can only 'make use' of what is earthly and temporal, for it has no lasting significance. As others have observed, conspicuously low in this mix is the Holy Spirit, our crucial bridge to the new Jerusalem. For we believe in angelic traffic between Dorset and the eternal city – and orbiting the Minster at Michaelmas is a wager on nothing less.

From the chained library

There is a gravity to our situation – and, being stuck to the ground, we are bound to myths of settlement and escape, adventure and return. We long both to exit and remain: this dynamic is written deep into our psyche and imagined places enable us to face it – simultaneously to land and transcend, a little lower than the angels.

Forty minutes from Wimborne is the ghost village of Tyneham, which there is time enough to visit before racing to Evensong in Salisbury. First, though, a quick tour of the Minster's interior, which forms an ascending stairway of lobes and levels – a brilliant mind inside a mundane body. Away from the mighty cloud of witnesses that gaze on while one celebrates Communion (among them King Ethelred of Wessex and the first Margaret Beaufort, grandmother of Henry Tudor), spiral steps rise to a cell-like chained library, founded by the rector, William Stone, in 1686. One of the first public libraries in the country, its books line up like convicts, whose ideas alone are allowed to break free.

The Minster is hard to leave. At length I see, set into the south-west wall, a colourful coffin, confining Anthony Etricke – notable local barrister and antiquary. The older (and, apparently, more 'humorous, phlegmatic and credulous') he grew, the more offended by his fellow townspeople he became, making a solemn vow that he 'would never be buried within the church or without it – neither below the ground nor above it'. Yet his irritation abated and Etricke then longed to be buried with his ancestors. To avoid breaking his oath, he therefore gained permission to make a recess in the wall where, Sunday by Sunday, his coffin awaited him, dated with the year – 1693 – that he confidently expected to bring promotion to glory. He lived on, however, until 1703, when the gold leaf numbers were carefully adjusted to display this delayed rapture. Whatever his shifting opinion of them, Anthony's neighbours evidently indulged and enjoyed their friend to the full.

Then, to Tyneham: somewhere I have been impatient to see since reading Patrick Wright's *The Village that Died for England*[37] – his brilliant, sceptical account of how this tiny Dorset community became emblematic of the nation's self-understanding since World War Two, when it was evacuated permanently by the Ministry of Defence. The unrequited campaign for its villagers to return home became, Wright argues, a nostalgic totem for politicians and writers shackled to a lost Eden, who 'arrive at their sense of English nationality by diminishment, fencing off the obtrusive modern world'. But today, those gates are open – on weekends, at least. Tyneham may be Imber's twin, but feels far less lost than the Wiltshire village, as is plain on my approach – joining the polite train of vehicles that descend into Worbarrow Bay by single-track tarmac, tucking into hedgerows every few yards for others to climb out and away.

Though still on army ranges, the cottages once blasted by tanks have been made secure, their rough ledges smoothed and strutted. There is a well-preserved parish church (closed for the pandemic), housing an exhibition about Tyneham's exiled villagers; there are numerous information boards and a restored K1 telephone box, with wartime advice crisply pasted inside. Less curated – and genuinely affecting, therefore – is the telegraph pole standing nearby. Insulators cracked and missing, its lack of wires a memorial to how stranded we are, how contact-less with the true past. 'So, *what* is this place?', one visitor asks another, as if to say they had imagined more.

Burn up the shocks

1662 Matins and the hollow tap of my footstep, climbing into a Jacobean pulpit whose stock is darkly carved with knots and nuts, like an oak tree. It really is a gorgeous box and entering the octagon I'm struck how each pulpit is a crow's nest on the sea of faith: a lookout for promised land. On occasion, also, wreckage you can cling to when your sermons run aground.

How many thousands of clerics have made this ascent before me? Unsteadily tripping on their robes, fumbling with a scant script, ready and unready for words of fire or folly to tumble out – forgettable tosh and (less often perhaps) electric truth that unexpectedly forms a circuit with those present: crackling, magically, into life.

This Wiltshire pulpit was installed at a point when the sermon was at the peak of its force in national propaganda and politics: when it was a despatch box – a matchbox, even, for the tinder of parliament against crown and the increasing heat of their friction; when, as John Chandos writes, 'a surplice was the most dangerous garment a man could own'. The greatest preachers of this incendiary age had a visceral power: witness this, Lancelot Andrewes's sermon from 1615, preached before the king in thanksgiving for deliverance from the Gunpowder Plot:

> Nay, would they make men's bowels fly up and down the ayr? Out with those bowels: what should they do in, that have not in them that that bowels should have. Would they do it by *fire*? Into the fire with their bowels, before their faces. Would they make mens *bones* fly about like *chips*? *Hew* their bones in sunder. Just as *Davids* prayer:

Their delight was in cruelty, let it happen to them; they loved not mercy, therefore let it be far from them.

This was the era when a special statute had to be raised to punish fighting in church: he who struck the first blow with a naked weapon should lose his ears or, 'if he wants ears', be branded on the face. When even a royalist archbishop like James Ussher could preach on the theme 'The natural man is a dead man', by reminding his white-knuckled congregants that 'the greatest man that lives cannot shield himself from a covering of worms' and dwelling with terrible care on the behaviours meriting eternal torment, and the 'filthy rabble' already headed there.

Eternity was, in the seventeenth century, a deeply politicized timeframe, and increasingly so as preachers amplified the monarch's claim to divine right in earthly governance, and ecclesiastical polity became, under William Laud, a vital means of retaining social order. In his sermon 'A Kingdom Melting', from the pivotal year of 1625, Laud presciently warns that, unless the king 'trust and indeere' his people and they, likewise, honour and obey their king, then 'in some degree or other there will bee *Liquefactio terra*, a *melting*, or a waste, both in Church and State'.

For many Puritans, of course, this was anathema – yet even their departure from this molten island was imbued with deep and regretful patriotism, as in Thomas Hooker's sermon of farewell to England, before leaving to found the colony of Connecticut. Citing Christ, weeping over Jerusalem, he mourns: 'God is going, his glory is departing, England hath seen her best days, and now evil days are befalling us: God is packing up his Gospell ...'

We naturally draw parallels with our own time – outlandishly different though the prologue to the English Revolution seems to us now. Yet the sense of impending chaos; a teetering desire to leave and begin again; our indignation, fear and frantic slicing of righteous from unrighteous: all these we recognize, as through a glass, darkly. So what place for the pulpit now, without the need to delay damnation – and when even those who believe in the eternal kind seem less inclined to give God's judgement a truly human face? At least the graphic hell of the seventeenth century felt physical, sensual – so close we might smell it, smouldering. I well recall Ralph Houlbrooke, Professor of Early Modern History at Reading (where I was an undergraduate), comparing these firebrands favourably to 'the kind of milk and water preaching we hear nowadays' and my strong disagreement, as I felt a vocation beginning to stir.

It was after the Restoration that sermons settled back into a more domestic tone – and Pepys could flit from pulpit to pulpit, taking them in, as if window displays. Then those Puritans who had lately burned up the shocks, like foxes in the Philistine fields, experienced their own exile: bound and sightless as Milton's Samson. Few public figures could survive the veering pandemonium of that era, although arguably the most golden-mouthed of them all managed to do so – Laud's protégé, Jeremy Taylor. Having been allowed to spend the Protectorate in Wales, far from Westminster, he preached with an unsurpassed lyricism, such that even his sinners went singing to their graves. In 'Of the Spirit of Grace', a sermon from 1651, he brings a Christlike lightness to the fetters of discipleship:

> And as no one will complain that their temples are restrained and their head is prisoner when it is encircled by a crown; so when the Son of God hath made us free, and hath only subjected us to the service and dominion of the Spirit, we are free as princes within the circles of their diadem, and our chains are bracelets ...

Taylor's facility was to make Godliness as winsome and desirable as worldly excess: it is the small pleasures, he says, that are the most delicious – 'the feeling of silke, or handling of a melon, or a moles skin'. Such is the kind of moderation we might die for. In our own disjointed times, likewise prone to fanatical extremes, Taylor can still coax us towards virtue. And though it seems unlikely the pulpit could regain its sentinel role in public affairs, we pressingly need those who can spy out the place to come and, furthermore, *describe* that land vividly enough for others to reach from the pew and grasp its shoreline. Preachers, in other words, who desire a better country – that is, a heavenly one.

Little Scotland

Past the plastic lions signing me to Longleat, I have skirted the estate to find Horningsham – home to the oldest non-conformist chapel in Britain. 'We invite you to come and worship' reads its noticeboard, Gothic script specked by a few dead flies scuttled in the casement. Sitting modestly under a bonnet of thatch, the present building originates from 1700, although the reputed date of its foundation, painted on to the east wall, is 1566.

Horningsham Chapel was provided by Sir John Thynne to accommodate Scottish labourers then employed in the creation of Longleat: first of the great 'prodigy houses' of

Elizabethan England and which, in turn, was built on the site of an Augustinian priory that Thynne had purchased after the Dissolution. These workmen lived on a street in the village still named Little Scotland, their meeting house a small colony of an altogether different kingdom.

Such tolerance looks genuinely exceptional for the times, given that uniformity in religion was such a vital sign of soundness in the body politic after the Elizabethan Settlement of 1559: fundamental to 'commonwealth', the period's favoured form of social imaginary. Setting the English situation in contradistinction to Catholic nations where Church and commonwealth were 'two societies independent', the Anglican architect Richard Hooker asserted that 'with us' these two were one. His justification drew deeply on the Old Testament vision – developed in the writings of Augustine – of divine reign over the nations of the earth and, moreover, godly princes who would enact the same: 'In a word,' he wrote:

> our estate is according to the pattern of God's own ancient elect people, which people was not part of them the commonwealth, and part of them the church of God, but the selfsame people whole and entire were both under one chief governor, on whose supreme authority they did all depend.

Likewise, John Jewel, Bishop of Salisbury: 'Queen Elizabeth doth as did Moses, Joshua, David ... and other godly emperors have done.' Recourse to these biblical antecedents would be a persistent theme throughout the following century, the 'Israel model' (as John Coffey describes it in his fine study *Persecution and Toleration in Protestant England 1558–1689*)[38] being fairly irresistible as a template for the nascent state Church – and, indeed, a justification for its violent persecution of those who chose not to belong. Recusancy, dissent, schism and heresy: all perforce became linked to political sedition.

The very founding figures who espoused a broad national Church confidently criminalized and imprisoned those whose consciences automatically made them enemies of the state: trapped like flies behind glass. Interrogating Henry Barrow, the leading Puritan Separatist who was consigned to London's pitiful Fleet prison, Lancelot Andrewes, future lyrical hand behind the King James Bible, commented, lightly: 'For close imprisonment you are most happie ... The solitarie and contemplative life I hold the most blessed life. It is the life I would chuse.' Denying himself, Andrewes opted instead to become Dean of Westminster: Barrow, meanwhile, was hanged.

Yet although Separatists continued to bear the brunt of intolerance, the irony was that most did not disagree with an 'Erastian' polity that ceded religious authority to civil powers. For Protestants of all kinds this was a logical extension not only of Old Testament kingship, but also the exacting standards of the New Testament Church towards false teaching and key Pauline texts such as Romans chapter 13, translated (under Andrewes's editorship) as, 'Let every soul be subject unto the higher powers. For there is no power but of God: the powers that be are ordained of God.' Far from objecting to temporal powers enforcing true religion, Puritans held rather that Anglicans had too roomy a view of who 'the elect' were – and so separated themselves for righteousness' sake.

The path towards toleration – especially of those perceived to be intolerant – was crazed with division, yet navigated at each stage by an emergent vision of Christian nationhood. Through the struggles of the English Revolution, the divine right of monarchy gradually transformed in popular conception to become the divine right of the nation – no less dangerous an idea, certainly, but one that injected a new and energetic sense of destiny into British foreign policy and the subsequent slow emergence of empire.

The same process, paradoxically enough, refined and

reinforced our most durable national value: individual liberty. When, three centuries later, Archbishop William Temple outlined three Christian social principles deriving from God's purposes in history, this one came first. To realize liberty is a political task; to conceive it a poetic and spiritual one. So it is worth recalling that the era's most impassioned and influential case for freedom of speech and expression came from the radical puritan John Milton, who envisaged a route through rigid conformity, on the one side, and 'many subdichotomies of petty schisms' on the other. Milton's *Areopagitica*, a polemic arising from the tempest of civil war, foresaw England liberated as 'a noble and puissant nation rousing herself like a strong man after sleep, and shaking her invincible locks'.

His earthly paradise was not pursued for long, however. Uniformity in religion (which returned with the invincible locks of Charles II) attempted once more to hold intact the cracked vessel of state, with common prayer its cementing agent. It is unsettling to know that the 1662 Prayer Book, daily mainstay of my own spiritual life, had such coercive political intent – which meant, among other things, that Horningsham Chapel was the closest place of worship its first recorded minister, Rowland Cotton, could walk to from his house in Warminster without conviction under the Five Mile Act. This last stage of the infamous Clarendon Codes – not repealed until 1828 – prevented dissenting clergy holding any other form of service within five miles of a town, where they might have 'oportunity to distill the poysonous Principles of Schisme and Rebellion into the hearts of His Majestyes Subjects to the great danger of Church and Kingdome'.

At this breeding ground of subversion today, they are gathering harvest gifts for the local food bank. Though I'm headed for the nearby town of Mere, there is time to peer inside and I'm thrilled to find the doors left unlocked. The chapel is gloriously untouched – pure, even – with looming Georgian pulpit and plain, panelled galleries. Over the entrance an ancient clock, long since stopped. I have no authority here but pad about guiltily, aware of the past I represent: in another age, I might have had them before the magistrate.

While the 1689 Toleration Act granted freedom of worship to all Protestant nonconformists (effectively as an acknowledgement of their loyalty during the succession of William and Mary), ongoing restriction from public office perpetuated these fault lines of discrimination and class. Not for the first time, I ask myself what it has done to the Anglican mind to have been for so long on the 'right' side of power and privilege – and whether our plausible inheritance may yet be redeemed.

Later on, at home, I consult Pevsner. 'Horningsham', he concludes, 'is a singularly loose village, with houses in their own gardens, small or large, and no visual cohesion.' He could be describing the United Kingdom. Better that, however, than to be bound as one with a tightness nobody can bear.

The Liberty of Ripon

At nine o'clock each evening in Ripon, North Yorkshire, the night-watch horn is blown, from each corner of the looming obelisk in the city square. This has happened, barring relocation during the pandemic (and, surely, other crises obscured by time), every evening since the ninth century, when Alfred the Great – a long way from Wessex – granted Ripon its charter and bestowed the horn as a security against the Viking raids then ravaging the north-east of England. Incredibly, this original charter horn, harbinger of darkness, remains in the town hall, where it is wrapped in black velvet and capped, like the night sky, with silver.

From the reign of Alfred's grandson, King Athelstan, until the advent of secular government in 1540, the entire city was protected by 'The Liberty of St Wilfrid', a city-wide sanctuary afforded to anyone entering within a mile of its boundary and marked by eight stone crosses. That peculiar status evolved into an independent legal system, which persisted until 1888 as The Ripon Liberty. The implications of being such an outlaw resort are thought-provoking to say the least, but reveal an idea, deeply founded in our culture, that every Christian settlement should also be a place of refuge. It would be fair to say that Britain, like most islands, has always been blurry about which new arrivals are invaders and which might be neighbours needing asylum.

Incomers for the day, we are paying a visit to Ripon's impressively preserved Workhouse Museum, which offers a fascinating index of our changing attitudes to welfare and belonging. Like many such institutions, this was recast in the 1930s as an old people's home – albeit with continuity of staff and inmates rechristened as residents. Thus it remained until 1976, after which the buildings became council offices and then, in 2017, a museum. What I find affecting is not so much the exhibits themselves (including, as expected, some stiffly grotesque dummies – such a staple of regional museums and invariably their most alarming feature), but the sense of a layout left starkly untouched: its casual ward for vagrants a corridor of tiny cells with a bleak and tapless bathing block that chills an already brisk October day.

The political debate that considered places like this in the first half of the nineteenth century oscillated between the benefits of local and national control. The ecclesiastical parish had looked after welfare of the poor since the time of Henry VIII and its relinquishment to regional boards of 'guardians' was seen by many at the time as an appalling stroke of centralization, outrage at which united old Tories and new radicals alike. The other balance to achieve was between the potentially conflicting obligations of charity and personal responsibility. Poverty was inescapably a matter of virtue and desert, and the 1834 report that framed the notorious 'New Poor Law' had a paranoia about encouraging idleness and vice, to the extent that it ended all 'outdoor' relief (that is, financial benefits, hitherto given to supplement low wages) and attempted to discourage pauperism by making 'well-regulated workhouses' as forbidding as possible. In this, at least, they succeeded. It was, accused Thomas Carlyle, 'a secret known to all rat-catchers: stop up the granary-crevices, afflict with continual mewing, alarm and going-off of traps [until] your "chargeable labourers" disappear and cease from the establishment'.

One of the most painful and abusive traps of Poor Law legislation was its understanding of 'settlement' – which, in various forms, tied the labourer to the parish of their birth and prevented them finding assistance elsewhere.

The extreme variance in parochial standards left many like spiders in a bathtub, unable to climb out and away from destitution.

'There is no touchstone, except the treatment of childhood,' wrote R. H. Tawney, 'which reveals the true character of a social philosophy more clearly than the spirit in which it regards the misfortunes of those of its members who fall by the way.' The issue of social welfare is always one of perception as much as policy: who is our neighbour and how do we see them? In an era when landed property was considered to be the very foundation of social order, Tawney explains that the landless poor were viewed as 'something less than a full citizen' – for what are they, who have nothing?

Those who possess the land are all too susceptible to an ancient and endemic lie (the correction of which underwrites the entire Old Testament), seducing them into thinking they are instruments, rather than objects, of God's judgement. To be reminded of this damnable mistake often takes a plague of sorts, although most of these still descend hardest of all on the poor. 'CHOLERA. Humiliation and Prayer' reads a printed notice from the mayor to the inhabitants of Ripon on the wall of the workhouse. From September 1849, it calls for the closing of shops and places of business, in order to turn in repentance to God in the face of 'a season of public affliction'.

Humiliation was already familiar to many, one suspects, in this threadbare sanctuary. I leave the place, unsettled. *As the night watch looks for the morning, so do we look for you, O Christ.*

CHOLERA.

Humiliation and Prayer.

TO THE

INHABITANTS OF THE BOROUGH OF RIPON.

Confident of your sympathy with me in the feeling that a season of Public affliction especially calls for the observance of the great Christian duties of Humiliation and Prayer, I beg leave to recommend the CLOSING of SHOPS, and PLACES of BUSINESS within the Borough, *on Wednesday next, the 26th Inst.,* (the day recommended by the Lord Bishop of the Diocese, for Religious observance) from half-past Nine o'clock in the Morning till One o'clock at Noon, and from Six o'clock in the Evening for the remainder of the day, in order to afford opportunities for *Public Worship, and Private Devotion.*

THOS. WILLIAMSON,
MAYOR.

Ripon, September 19th, 1849.

THIRLWAY AND SON, PRINTERS, RIPON.

How the land lies

Half term, and a few days' release under the vast skies of the Isle of Arran. I was last here on a family holiday in 1977, the week Elvis Presley died: our febrile Austin Maxi overheating as we rushed for the ferry in a fluster of roadside steam. Gazing out upon the sea's silver jubilee, a memory bubbles up from that distant fortnight – of the local paper, *The Arran Banner*, fulminating that a brick had been thrown through their office window, wrapped in a note complaining at the lack of punk rock coverage in their editorial. My brothers and I found this ludicrous even then, so I was glad on arrival to find the *Banner* still in circulation and resolutely upholding its musical embargo over forty years on.

Capsule-shaped, like a human head, Arran appeals by accommodating to the imagination. Covering an area roughly that of Glasgow, but with only two principal roads – one a coastal circuit, the other a bisection of its highland and lowland halves – the island is small enough to know intimately, while large enough to feel untamed and remote. In the 1970s, bikers from the mainland would set up semi-permanent camps on the beaches; our taxi driver was one of them – newly landed from thirty years on the rigs and yearning to be stranded on Arran again, with just a tent and the scent of two-stroke.

Drawn by the promise of log fires, wine and wilderness, we came to see family in their gently decomposing farmhouse at Blackwaterfoot, along the western shore of the island. Among these attractions was the prospect of locating the rocks known as Hutton's Unconformity, which may be found jutting like an orthodontic problem from the coastline near our former holiday home at Lochranza. As its name indicates, the Unconformity is a break, a disruption: a liminal point where two divergent types adjoin, and the crooked strata here mark one of several Scottish sites where the geologist James Hutton discerned the deep, shifting processes involved in land formation. His visit to Arran in 1787 marked another epiphany in an era busily keen to see the world anew – and, by so doing, as more ancient than had ever been supposed.

Having reached the outcrop along a shingle path – its colliding chevrons clearly visible (albeit not dramatic enough to inspire one's shivering children) – we returned for an evening of card games and books. Too parochial and preoccupied with England, some cross-border perspective was long overdue, so I pulled down *The Highland Clearances*: John Prebble's vivid (if not uncontested) account of the enforced desertion of highland communities already underway when Hutton was hammering the schist on Arran.

The most striking impression left by this book is of contrasting forms of 'landedness': that of the clan chiefs and (often English) aristocracy – to whom the land belonged, yet who appear curiously disconnected from it – and their people, presented in mystic unity with a shared soil of which they owned not an inch. For Prebble, a communist, this was deeply significant. Like most historians, he found in the past what he was looking for – which is not to say that it wasn't really there, merely to affirm that we perceive those aspects of the truth that our traditions attune us to. The land itself equivocates, and sometimes bears false witness.

Nevertheless, even this far south there is evidence of a seismic social shift, discounted for generations until Prebble and others had the eyes to see it. Just down from Lochranza there is a ridge of whitewashed cottages known as The Twelve Apostles, built to rehouse resistant islanders who, replaced on the hillsides by deer, now had to fish for their lives. Predictably enough, the parish church was complicit in this upheaval. The patronage system, whereby landowners would appoint malleable ministers, inevitably meant the muting of a more radical voice, one that would eventually be liberated when the Free Church of Scotland split with the established denomination in 1843. During the Clearances it seems as though the main role of the parish minister was to lend moral support, seasoned with eternal threat, to the uprooting process.

Here on Arran, unconformity again broke the surface in 1815, with the appointment by the Duke of Hamilton of a Reverend Crawford: full of years but apparently little else to his credit. Crawford's flock deserted the kirk faster than they had the hills, setting up an unofficial alternative in what became known as 'The Preaching Cave', just along the coast from Blackwaterfoot. Learning of this on our last morning, I scrambled down the shore in search of where these irregular worshippers had met and found there a deep, prismatic recess scoured from the cliffs in whose dripping chancel, dressed with fishing net, leant a driftwood cross – juncture of opposites.

Speenhamland

In the rain-glossed streets of Speenhamland this morning. Such an appealing name, yet this place I've imagined as a nation entire of itself has long been subsumed into the town of Newbury – once an essential staging post on the route from London to Bath. Past a dreary-looking Job Centre Plus (its green and yellow sign sun-bleached and well overdue for rebranding), to find the building that – as the George and Pelican Inn – was one of the most prestigious pubs in the country. Nelson's favoured stop-off, and of royalty and politicians, it was here in 1795 that the notorious 'Speenhamland' system of local welfare was devised by Berkshire magistrates, which became synonymous with pauperizing whole swathes of rural society.

The simple idea was to supplement the low wages of hired labourers, newly reliant on relief following the wholesale enclosure of common land, with poor-law allowances that would vary according to the price of bread and the size of each labourer's family. The net effect, however, was to entrap most working households in a benefit system they could not escape, tied as it was to the settlement laws binding them to their parish. It was from this cage that the New Poor Law of 1834 sought to deliver them – while in practice merely switching one form of penury for another: the workhouse.

Parochial relief, in one form or another, has been at the heart of local welfare in England for centuries. The Tudor Poor Laws, by which the parish church was made an enduring instrument of the state, refined the medieval compact of community and charity that religious life had long offered (via church or monastery), enduing

143

parish officers with new civil authority. Parsons had to be present at whippings of 'rogues and vagabonds' and also, by statute, 'exhort, move, stir and provoke people to be liberal' – a conflicting moral stance, to say the least, yet powerful enough still to need satirical demolition by Dickens 300 years later.

The story of the Church of England's involvement in welfare is also an account of the changing role and reach of the state and its special relationship with Christianity – of which the government's current distinction between the Church's worship and its welfare work is but the freshest expression. Proposals now being considered in Whitehall for a new 'social covenant' with faith groups, that they might undertake to provide at the local level certain aspects of social policy, represents a strikingly sixteenth-century response to twenty-first-century challenges: not unwelcome, but one that begs awareness of an extremely long cautionary tale.

The drift towards greater centralization took place incrementally, almost accidentally. A rapid and massive increase in population and urbanization altered everything, demanding more of parish governance than it could supply. Inevitably, parish vestries evolved into local corporations as recognizably modern forms of local government took shape. While parish rule was defended as 'the glory of Englishmen', the plain fact was that an increasingly complex society demanded more bureaucracy, both locally and nationally. Against their political instincts, which in the nineteenth century favoured self-help, individual freedom and minimal intervention by government into such liberties, those in government nevertheless saw little option but to augment the powers of the secular state.

This may not have been a lack of political imagination (the Victorians were not wanting in that respect) but arguably of trust. Emerging positions on both Right and Left increasingly saw the remedy of social ills being most safely dispensed at a national level, and localism as unreliable and archaic – which in many respects it had proved to be. The parochial basis of welfare gave way to the nation, with the 1662 Act of Settlement finally being repealed with the Welfare State legislation of 1948.

Though arrived at with horse-drawn slowness, the post-war settlement of the Attlee government was a pivotal shift in the country's centre of gravity. For the majority of the rural population, especially, the parish boundary had, for centuries, held far more relevance and direct impact upon their lives than that of the nation. Speenhamland was England – largely because mobility (then, as now) came with money and any escape from settlement tended to leave the poor behind. The social historian Frank Prochaska has called the Anglican Church's withdrawal from statutory (though by no means voluntary) social service 'an abdication of a historic responsibility', whereafter the poor belonged not first to their community, but to the state.

It would be easy to attribute this change to the Christian socialism of William Temple, from whose mouth the phrase 'Welfare State' was first coined. Yet his political position was, both in theory and practice, less statist and more Burkean than is sometimes assumed. Principally this is because it was grounded in Anglican doctrine, which begins with God located in Christ. Particular to universal – and not the other way around – is the grain of Christian theology, and so Temple's stance is poised between the need for central control and local freedom. He wrote in *Christianity and Social Order* (his wartime manifesto for change):

> Most political theories confine attention to the individual and the state as the organ of the national community; they tend to ignore the intermediate groupings. But that makes any understanding of actual liberty impossible; for it exists in the most part in and through those intermediate groups – the family, the church, or congregation,

the guild, the Trade Union, the school, the university ...
Liberty is actual in the various cultural and commercial
and local associations that men form.[39]

The drift towards centralization perceived in both Church
and state today is, like that of the nineteenth century,
largely ungoverned by ethics – being more our pragmatic
response to an increasingly complex and connected society.
Next to the George and Pelican Inn is a small square plaque
indicating that 'The first official mobile telephone call in
the UK was made to Vodafone offices close to this site on
1st January 1985'. The old parochialism had unravelled
long before: probably around the time the inn closed in the
1850s once the railway made stagecoaches unnecessary.
But a new kind is vital if we are to recover our balance,
our compass and our belonging. Neither Universal Credit
in our own day nor its particular historic counterpart in
the relief of Speenhamland may in themselves hold the
answer to welfare without attending to what is primary –
our fellowship with the poor, which must be real and not
remote. For theirs, after all, is the kingdom to come.

Torn loaf

The land around Avebury is warty with barrows and burial mounds. Most are brushed with trees and now, in November, these stand in bristling outline against the sky. I walk up here just before dawn, hungry for the half-light that lends a mystical blur to the plainest journey.

This suits the start of the day, when I am by no means bright – thoughts coalescing slowly like ancient plates. After a mile or two, islands of clarity have begun to emerge: liberated, paced out. If God may be known as both act and being, our prayers must, I think, attempt a similar balance. Seeing the soupiness of my early devotions when sitting at home, I now tend to get moving and leave the stillness till evening.

The Wessex landscape is no older than any other bit of Britain: it is just that prehistory here lies so close to the surface – uninterred, or uninterrupted by later accretions – so the genius of this place is more evidently ancient. In the estates of south-east London, I needed an urban theology: now I am faced with something far less concrete.

So a little distance from the Ridgeway on the western slope of Overton Hill, I climb a trinity of barrows and give praise to the Godhead, treading up and down with each hump in the liturgy. The labour of those lines: '*Glory* to the Father, *and* to the Son ... *and* to the Holy Spirit' is eased, made musical, by such motion. Cresting one mound, I find a single cracked stone: altar to an unknown deity. Two sections, arranged together, their break is like a lightning bolt or split cell – a telling image for today when my mind is filled with portents of division in the Church. For we appear once again to be on the verge of a kind of meiosis over sexual ethics: ironic, given that it concerns an act of union wherein our being reaches for its dimly recalled oneness with another.

This is, of course, also about God – who, unobjecting, allows himself to be grappled over like the infant before Solomon. Would that wise king actually have allowed such a slicing, do you wonder? There was a gamble there, a bid for good sense and genuine love to appear. No relenting in Jesus' case, however, who is a man possessed, pressed into marriage with our every claim and cause. Mute before their shrieking, he is presented again: the torn loaf, for a world that refuses to be but partly right.

Behind the clustered beeches a purpling robe of sky, the rising day.

God's acre

Into the winter mist, with Wiltshire crisp as Christmas. Green and tan-toned fields by the Bath Road have turned silver and fawn with an Advent frost, and I am puffing along the track beyond Avebury's Stone Avenue to where Silbury Hill rises from the ground, as if forced up by enormous moles.

Over 4,000 years from its construction (to no apparent purpose – not that artistry needs any other), Silbury still looks artificial: patted from a basin or slapped out by plastic spades. In fact, it is calculated that this unique Neolithic pudding took some four million working hours to create, across several generations. And though staying put, pert in the landscape, it's an elusive thing – in and out of sight, crouched beside the undulating A4. Oddly hard to photograph, I find – and best viewed from here on the neighbouring slope, where November sunlight now leaks lemony through the fog.

Silbury Hill has a broad, moating border that stayed flooded until the spring. Dry so far (despite the swelling Winterbourne nearby), while I watch, this ditch fills with a filmy collar that leaves the flat top clear, as if for performance. A local band, pleading ignorance of the ban on people climbing it, played there a couple of years back and it's easy to see why – being a stage like no other. A friend who was stationed here for National Service in the 1950s, at nearby RAF Yatesbury, recalls shinning up, as everyone did until fairly recently when fears for the mound's erosion stopped all that. It now sits, sacrosanct – which I think a pity.

Thirty-five years ago, in his book *On Living in An Old Country*, Patrick Wright observed the process by which Britain in the twentieth century commodified and circumscribed national history, culminating in the National Heritage Act of 1983, from which English Heritage was formed. 'National Heritage', he writes:

> involves the extraction of history – of the idea of historical significance and potential – from a denigrated everyday life and its restaging or display in certain sanctioned sites, events, images and conceptions.[40]

While it is easy to overstate this change – in many ways vital for the preservation of such sites – it has involved a new kind of enclosure of what was formerly common land. Even when releasing private property into public ownership, this has inevitably brought new demarcations and discontinuities of space and time that elevate the past into another realm and make it less reachable, somehow. Which is precisely the debate now digging in around the mooted Stonehenge tunnel, half an hour south of Silbury Hill. To what extent we trespass upon the past is a matter of secular holiness – in other words, which everyday things do we set apart and how far should we take that consecration?

Given that the Church of England possesses such a large proportion of the country's historic buildings – the vast majority of which still house living communities of faith unbroken since their foundation – the way in which we own and inhabit our heritage (and continue to pay for it) is for me a grave and urgent concern. Churches were already set apart – 'God's Acre' in the Christian idiom – but in a way that drew others into their sacred space, even where railed off. As a child in Luton, after Sunday services I would hide under the high altar (a hefty concrete henge in a breeze-block building), quite at home behind the antependia. Now that the heritage value of smaller places of worship is increasingly recognized – and, like cathedrals before them, the local church negotiates the awkward boundary, turnstiled by admission fees, between visiting and devotion – the right to belong in our past must include the right to interfere with it: to tread upon and thereby alter what is ours, for the present.

Whether or not Silbury Hill was once a place of worship we won't ever know – though this seems probable, given its situation amid what is now the Avebury World Heritage Site. Equivalent in height and volume to the Egyptian pyramids (with which it is contemporary), I love that this extraordinary heap is, despite everything, so neighbourly and self-effacing. Look to one side when driving by or – like the disconnected past – you might just miss it.

Leper windows

Muddy skies and a dun-coloured day. Grubs of spray fleck the screen on the morning college run, as Grace tells how a raucous passenger, sitting behind her on yesterday's bus, cussed the pandemic and all those crowding too closely about her. Obscuring herself behind the convenient wall of her art portfolio, she sank into her seat and the sanctuary of headphones. There'll be more room, she hopes, on this morning's slow coach to Trowbridge.

The past year has rearranged perceptions of space and place in ways that will keep anthropologists tapping out theses for some time to come. Our sense of personal boundary, so implicitly policed, is being renegotiated, perhaps permanently – and, as always, this holds real ethical and spiritual significance. Separation, set-apartness, is inherently linked to both health and holiness: to the concepts of pollution and taboo that Mary Douglas explored in her 1966 book *Purity and Danger*.[41] Fear of defilement or infection is central to the way in which all cultures keep particular things and people at arm's length, or far further. Yet any functioning society, Douglas concludes, must also learn to integrate the contradictions of material life and death, and dwell with mortality's contamination, like the ash-stain on a Lenten forehead or St Francis of Assisi, lain naked on the soil as his hour approached.

While we instinctively keep a Levitical distance from corruption and impurity, true sanctity is much messier, mingling the categories we normally impose. Witness the centuries of dispute about the nature of Christ in the early Church, from which the creeds emerged: the problem of whether his divinity and humanity were distinct essences, test-tubed in antithesis, or could blend in some way, infusing each other as whisky through water. This took so long to resolve – remaining suspended in a solution of words – because Jesus Christ was really the human question in concentrate. For those who would keep God like one at risk, remote in a well-swept heaven, the blood-sweating Nazarene is a discomfiting riposte. Women and men closest to him have tended to find themselves impelled ever further into the world's dirtier places.

This present distance cannot last because it is, we sense, deeply inhuman. In the midst of death, we must be in life – and the impulse driving us over this boundary is no more or less than charity. Charity gets soiled, not set apart, and genuine care has about it a degree of care-freedom, if not carelessness. The challenge now before us is to find ways of being thus engaged in adventurous love, while avoiding the folly of laying down our friends' lives for our own.

At early nightfall, I cross Wiltshire again to find the former plague village of Broughton Gifford, delighted to be out and leading a service for the first time in weeks. The homes here are strung out like garments on a line, the lane unlit and pitted with black puddles. Hauling my vestments into church, I am shown in the porch a row of four panes like portholes, ancient and pleasingly uneven. These are, I learn, leper windows: affording access to those kept apart from the community by sickness. Imagine such faces, greyed out and ghostly, pressing into the frames while others drew near! These windows have stayed and played on my mind in the two days since. Maybe, a friend reflects, they could be beautified or filled with stained glass as a testimony to this extraordinary, suspended year – small lights for the isolated.

The green stick

To arise, creaking, from my desk and head across the Plain to Warminster yesterday was a welcome escape. I have been folded in an s-shape all week – shoulders hunched, legs tucked back into my stool – and, while the day was dreich, I felt unfurled.

On the radio as I splashed across the county, Mark Carney, the former Governor of the Bank of England, was delivering the first of his Reith Lectures: 'How we get what we value'.[42] Having looked forward to a music podcast saved for the journey, I was nevertheless held to the end by his erudition and humanity. Carney was posing the question as to whether the inexorable shift from market economy to market society has devoured the very social capital on which all resources – human, economic and natural – depend. In negating the moral foundations that Adam Smith saw as vital for the market to thrive, he was asking whether capitalism had not, in fact, consumed itself.

As the programme ended, I parked up at St Aldhelm's, Bishopstrow: one of relatively few churches dedicated to the legendary eighth-century scribe and first Bishop of Sherborne. Immediately inside are two stained windows celebrating tales of Aldhelm: one in which King Ine of Wessex offers his own staff to the saint, promising him land for a church to the extent he can throw it (one, possibly far-fetched, origin of 'Bishopstrow') and another in which the saint's crozier has turned into an ash tree, the story being that he preached for so long that his staff, placed on the nearby ground, took root – hence, 'Bishop's tree'.

My own is in the car, slung between the handbrake and the boot, but I like the latter tale best. And I wonder, what could it mean in such a mobile age for us to live a planted life – so sown that we might flourish into leaf? It is too easy to be romantic about pre-industrial England, when the norm was (as Peter Laslett puts it in *The World We Have Lost*) 'stable poverty' for most – and any settled account must balance benefit with cost.[43] But what seems clear is that the uprooting of market economics has, when fully grown, detached commercial life from the local and household origins implicit in *oikonomia*.

This is what the guild socialists of the early twentieth century were seeking to retrieve: economics at a human and communal scale, in which the perceived medieval embedding of trade within place, faith and family could offer an alternative to the machines of capitalism and communism, both of which turned people into commodities.

The familiar narrative is that The Reformation – by privatizing religion and keeping the kingdom of heaven far from this world – brought about the divorce of what Carney referred to as 'the Magi and the merchant', to a degree that would be inconceivable to our medieval forebears. The creation of the Bank of England in 1694 by Act of Parliament arguably enshrined this unmooring of commerce from social and theological context – although, as R. H. Tawney (whose 1926 opus *Religion and the Rise of Capitalism* is still such a fluent and useful book) put it:

> a philosophy which treated the transactions of commerce and the institutions of society as indifferent to religion would have appeared [to those in former centuries], not merely morally reprehensible, but intellectually absurd.[44]

But it does not seem absurd now, which is ironic since, as Mark Carney observes, our unquestioned belief in the supremacy of the market, monetizing all other values, has entered the realm of faith. For him – as for many other commentators – the environmental crisis is what will force a new kind of Reformation, upturning the old financial certainties.

It must by now be unquestionable that ecology will redefine economy in the twenty-first century. Yet the spirituality of that shift is still very much an open and thereby competitive market, in which the prevailing response is to repeat our former mistake of abstracting universal ideals from their particular tradition. Given that both 'economy' and 'ecology' signify the value of home, our social ethics must likewise land in time and place. The ways that endure will be those with the deepest roots.

The Cuckoo Stone

Winter solstice this week, with bollards blocking each parking space on the approach to Stonehenge. Undeterred, ancient Transits and ersatz campers of various kinds have nosed into improbable berths around the Plain – as at Avebury, further north, whose status is likewise elevated for the festival. I'm driving from one to the other at six-thirty, the morning thick and dark as ink, to meet with a friend for an early walk.

Louis and I plan to explore the land around Durrington Walls, a ridge-like earthwork thought to have housed the Neolithic navvies who constructed Stonehenge, as long before the first Christmas as we are after it. In the last two years this area has once again become a building site, with the busy expansion of Larkhill to house thousands of military personnel rebased from Germany. These fields – where, incidentally, The Beatles filmed a couple of breezy numbers in the Salisbury Plain sequence of *Help!*, Chieftain tanks and Eleanor Bron disporting about them – are newly street-lit, with a glossy carapace of tarmac and pristine red brick.

We begin at Woodhenge: another circular shrine pegged out in low stumps, resembling a children's playground or contemporary sculpture. Some years ago, the split skull of an infant was found interred at its centre, suggesting a ritual purpose too grisly to contemplate. Goodness only knows how our ancestors lived, when all we have is cracked bones and guesswork. The sky now bluestone-grey, we traipse through the drizzle towards King Barrow Ridge, a line of burial mounds providing the closest vantage point for viewing Stonehenge without paying an entry fee. Louis – from a farming family and far more confident than I am around cattle – concedes to skirt a scruffy group of heifers and rejoin the route at a point where a lone, prone sarsen punctuates the path. Known as the Cuckoo Stone, and formerly raised erect, it is one of the only boulders of such size to be found on the Plain. The sole feature in a broad field, it looks curiously out of place – as if inadvertently dropped on the way.

Conversation finds its range when walking, and (among lighter themes) we home in on Christianity as an inherited thing, and its particular association with the English landscape. However vague and variegated our personal beliefs, parish churches remain both physically and imaginatively attached to the national scene, their buildings embodying the less visible filaments of faith. I confess my devotion to this archetype and the ease with which it assumes possession – of territory, of history, and of the countryside, especially. I admit my fear of losing place and being unable to pass on intact what was handed down to me. Being, I suspect, precisely the kind of religious leader Christ confronted with the need to prise their fingers from the kingdom, I am challenged again to relinquish my belongings.

Yet this land never did belong to Anglicans, so much as we to it – bound by a kind of specific gravity. A commitment, a cure. In Scripture, land is viewed through the prism of *promise*, whereby the longing for a human home is locally mediated before its heavenly consummation. The New Testament, for all it reorientates the Abrahamic covenant around the person of Jesus, does not spirit us away into paradise: heirs of Christ (St Paul writes) are like Isaac, children of that same, grounded assurance. And if the inspiration for English nationhood was the biblical Israel, a paramount question for churches here (as in any country thus formed) must be: *What now for our covenant with this place?*

A degree of exile is vital in order to see this afresh – not least to return us to a more radical vision that puts the land in the hands of the dispossessed. For the meek are blessed when the mighty are put down from their seat and the proud scattered for their failure of imagination. What, then, would it mean for those on the outside, whose tenuous stake in society has been further weakened by Covid-19, to find their place in a reunited kingdom? To seek this better country, Mary must be the new model of power: the Magnificat our manifesto.

Wiltshire's gift this morning is its reminder that any tenure here is temporary, a leasehold at most: and this nest we have built must inevitably be supplanted, as we have supplanted others. Property, after all, is a form of trespass when your true footing is in heaven. Sipping from a flask of soapy coffee on the miniature hills of King Barrow Ridge, we see at last the outline of Stonehenge, just yards from a stream of brake lights sequinning the A303 (soon also to be buried if the proposed tunnel goes ahead). I love this turf. But the earth is the Lord's, the Psalmist sings, and not because we claim or colonize it for him but because God is its source, its founder – among us in Christ as one cast aside, like a discarded rock.

- stone is out of place though now part of the landscape.

- metaphor of the church...
  ~~God~~ in the communal of the community. "

O Radix

Mistletoe nests are an arresting sight, set high in a winter tree: alien enough to draw me into a makeshift layby and gaze dizzily up to where they blot and cluster the boughs. Late in Advent, I'm following the Avon south to Fordingbridge along the border of the diocese, for a few festive visits. A bottle on a doorstep; a porchway prayer. Over the rusting scrub of Hale Purlieu, the New Forest has an entirely different complexion from my usual chalk downland: I feel like a tourist here, passing through.

We have Pliny the Elder to thank for the association of oak-mistletoe with druidic practice, his *Natural History* referring to its ceremonial gathering with a gold sickle by white-robed priests, whose cloaks cupped the apparently rootless sprigs so they would not touch the ground, remaining suspended between heaven and earth. It was this single reference that the eighteenth-century antiquarian and Anglican clergyman William Stukeley (who saw druids on these plains as readily as Blake viewed angels in Peckham) adopted and amplified in his narrative, wherein such foundling clerics became patriarchal forerunners of English Christianity, with mistletoe – because of its mystical provenance and unusual growth in winter – 'a type of the expected messiah'.

Whether or not it be the golden bough of mythology, mistletoe is by no means miraculously begotten or self-sustaining, but parasitic: drawing moisture from the host tree, which it slowly weakens. It is (as Geoffrey Grigson observed in his indispensable study of plant lore, *The Englishman's Flora*) essentially 'an excrescence', drawing on roots not its own. As such, it makes a metaphor of sorts for Anthropocene culture, when harmful human impact upon the environment has grown apace with our spiritual and commercial detachment from the soil. Unfettered consumption has been a powerful aphrodisiac – magical, even, in effect. But the existential threat from living as if we floated above the earth is one we now feel keenly, like the slicing December wind.

Jesus (John the Baptist cried) was an axe, poised at the base of a fruitless trunk. And while the Nativity places the Christ-child deep in his Jewish ancestry – 'a rod out of the stem of Jesse', as Isaiah has it, and 'a branch out of his roots' – the New Testament holds the radical promise that those who have no such footing may find everlasting life when grafted into his stock.

In the Sarum Rite – the Latin liturgy developed at Salisbury Cathedral and used in its worship between the Norman Conquest and the Reformation – each of the seven days before Christmas Eve was marked by an antiphon calling upon Christ to lead and deliver his people. Stopping by on my way home, I ask the masked guides to point me towards a medieval window containing, I have read, some of the oldest 'historiated' stained glass in the country. Though dulled by time and low light, I can just make out the snaking lines of a thirteenth-century Jesse Tree, depicting Jesus' earthly genealogy. Halfway up, the Saviour sits among its branches, his garment green as an apple.

> O Root of Jesse,
> Standing as a sign among the peoples;
> Before you kings will shut their mouths,
> To you the nations will make their prayer:
> Come and deliver us, and delay no longer.

Their country, by another road

Silver morning, sliding lane. Brittle panes of ice glaze every puddle – larger ones wheezing with my foot's irresistible step. Cracks snap out like lightning, in little branches. Our land is frost-smitten, and all things formerly unstuck now have a new bond, stiffly cemented as one.

Epiphany has returned, whose purpose is to admit the unexpected – charlatan guests, alternate routes, tyranny thwarted by the year's pulsing infant light. I'm up on Chute Causeway, taking my daily allotment of liberty. Past the collapsed long barrow at Tidcombe, plundered for its treasures in the eighteenth century, and away to the county border with Hampshire. This is deep, game-keeper countryside, but the road is an old and important one, part of the Roman way from Winchester to Cunetio, a major settlement now buried under a bland field near Marlborough. Roman roads are a vital component in Christian history, the means by which apostles – and their epistles – could move safely and swiftly around the ancient world. Ours was principally a metropolitan religion, strid-ing from city to city, such that when the Empire adopted Christianity (ushering churches, erstwhile poachers, on to their estate), those who maintained the old practices came to be known as *pagani* – rustic villagers, off-roaders.

This stretch of their old straight track has some striking signs of an origin around that time. Burnt ash or powder was found in quantities beneath the upper layers, indi-cating (it is thought) the residue of fires lit on the flint foundation to make beacons that would smoke-sign the path when laying out the road ahead. Visible beside the blacktop this morning are deep-green trenches, which are possible quarry pits dug for its construction when the legions were still stationed here, in Britannia Superior. But Chute Causeway is a bit different: one of the only lengths of Roman road that veers off course – for four miles, in a great sweeping bend. It does so to avoid a deep coombe that, presumably, proved too great an obstacle to navigate.

The view this morning is murkily beautiful, and bitingly cold – the right kind of mood for a tale told about this section of the Causeway, concerning a former Rector of Vernham Dean, a small parish not far ahead. During the reign of Charles II, at the height of the plague, the priest persuaded villagers to isolate themselves, away from their dwellings in an encampment at the top of the hill, assuring them he would regularly supply provisions and bring them himself. Fearing contagion, though, the story goes that he refused to deliver the gifts, leaving his people to perish. Dying of the disease himself soon after (assumed to be a grim kind of justice, in that odd way we attribute partiality to infection, which was ever even-handed), he is thought to haunt the road yet, determinedly trying to bring the relief he failed to in life: walking towards his terrors.

Whatever happened – and something of the kind probably did – we mutter a prayer for the poor fellow, and hope he hears. Fearful slips are easily made in such off-kilter months, calling on every camelled reserve as we swerve uncertainly home.

On Liddington Hill

Our love of the land is unrequited. Though responding when we tend, delve or hack, it is indifferent as to who does this and careless if they do not. Eve and Adam may fondly have named the species – each foxglove, fern and butterfly – but those species did not name us back. So while imagining a barley field bowed under the wind to be praising its maker, it is only we who see the suggestion, who decorate the earth with personality.

First light, on Liddington Hill, having learned it was the site of Richard Jefferies's boyhood epiphany – when, in 1866, gazing out on oceanic downland, that son of Swindon was overwhelmed by the sunlit summit and felt 'an emotion of the soul beyond all definition', as if addressed, caressed by creation. Even through winter mist, with the M4 roaring invisibly below, it remains majestic: close to the Ridgeway and crowned by one of the country's oldest hill forts. Slithering my car on to a verge (and trusting it won't slump back while I'm gone) I puff up the track like a tank engine before reaching a beech clump that marks the hill for miles along the motorway. This viewpoint has grown into an unofficial shrine for the departed, with wilting stems and votive tokens scattered about – even small plaques tacked on to the trees. Every leaf bristles with loss, and the cost of living.

Liddington Camp became sacred ground for Richard Jefferies, whose favoured place in the current renaissance of nature writing is, I suspect, partly due to this transparent desire to know the earth by heart. His prose style is measured and modern – never florid or self-important, but almost clerical in recording each scene. Edward Thomas rightly observed that his words 'call no attention to themselves', for the land is what Jefferies wanted us to see: to feel as he did its pulsing presence and count its alluring ways.

Following a permissive path past blue-daubed sheep leads to the castle – or at least its cratered imprint. A good – if gusty – spot to reflect upon Jefferies's life and the leitmotifs that lift him above the ordinary. His varied body of work was a romance with nature in which the author could not help returning to the question of whether he was beheld as well as beholding – his locus, as it were, in the world's affections.

In his children's tale *Wood Magic*, whose protagonist evokes Jefferies's own wandering boyhood, the youth finds himself able to speak with the elements and animals and be addressed by them. Asked to explain its song, a brook responds with a soliloquy on existence, relating how an eternal current runs through nature. 'There is no such thing as time', it tells him. 'That which has gone by, whether it happened a second since, or a thousand years since, is just the same; there is no real division betwixt you and the past.'[45] Here is a true slice of Wessex philosophy – the ancient made ever new, dismissing as too light a thing the inconvenient centuries.

Jefferies's own beliefs evaded the usual religious defin-itions. While able to write luminously about his childhood parish church at Chiseldon (in which he sits 'until the mind is magnetized by the spirit of the past'), at core Jefferies worshipped life itself – the mystery of being – which, ultimately, seemed unable to respond. This lends an acute and peculiar poignancy to his final writings. In a last testament of faith (*The Story of My Heart*), the ailing author, not yet forty, firmly refuses to afford per-sonality to the material world. 'There is nothing human in nature', he asserts: 'The earth, though loved so dearly, would let me perish on the ground and neither bring forth food nor water.' Indeed, he calls the universe 'distinctly anti-human', concluding that 'no deity has anything to do with nature', which is 'a force without a mind'. His own mortality in view, Jefferies declines to scan the horizon for signs of God. But what if the kingdom of heaven was within? What if, as that earlier poet of Wiltshire, George Herbert, put it in his poem 'Providence':

> Of all the creatures both in sea and land
> Only to Man thou hast made known thy ways,
> And put the pen alone into his hand,
> And made him Secretary of thy praise.

> Man is the world's high Priest: he doth present
> The sacrifice for all; while they below
> Unto the service mutter an assent,
> Such as springs use that fall, and winds that blow.[46]

I leave Liddington Hill, wondering whether Jefferies's self-less devotion to these fields diverted his gaze away from the very role he fulfilled so eloquently. In clear-eyed insist-ence that the earth must not be confused or conflated with God, he stands in contrast to the Gaia-shaped spirituality of contemporary environmentalism, which tends to ascribe divinity either to everything or to nothing at all.

The biblical record, so formative of the Western attitude to nature, viewed matter differently. Creation was distinct from God, yet adored by him: its stewardship being entrusted to humanity. Addressing an exiled and desolate nation, Isaiah prophesies that the land will no longer be termed 'Forsaken' but renamed 'Beulah' – married to the Lord. For a race estranged from Eden, Christ comes as the New Adam, to restore that bond as both lover and beloved. On Easter morning, bleary with grief, Mary mistakes him for a gardener.

'Hours of Spring' is probably the last essay Richard Jefferies composed with his own hand, far from his precious home county, barely able to lift a pen through infirmity, and it expresses his despair at nature's thoughtless continuity beyond his brief span: 'A thousand thousand buds and leaves and flowers and blades of grass, things to note day by day, increasing so rapidly that no pen can put them down ... All these without me – how can they manage without me?' His fountain of words has meant they do not, entirely.

Nearly nine o'clock, and I must be back. At the edge of Liddington copse is a large concrete pillbox – used as a control room during World War Two for the 'Starfish' decoy operations held on this hilltop. Designed to deflect enemy bombers from the railway junctions at nearby Swindon, these involved sparking a complex array of incendiary devices that produced a spectacular mock inferno. It worked, apparently, allowing at least a partial passover. What life must have been like up here in those nights – behind the blast doors of this artificial hell – is something I've dwelt on all week. That, and the secluded shrine skirted on my way down, where yelling need can be flung at the unfeeling sky.

Gleba

Little to glean from the last fortnight, it feels. The fields have been unphotographable: drably damp, footpaths lathered with mud. Nature is still in retreat and, with my advance, pheasants snap fatly into flight and a myopic smudge of hare heads, as ever, in the opposite direction. But this morning, at last, a frost – and the scene is renewed, sending me gleefully out. There is a mania to photography, which I find troubling in a low-key way, for you become greedy for views, snatching at the sunrise and swishing at the air like a naturalist with a net. All collectors should regularly let things go: unhooking one perfect catch in seven, so as to control their desire for capturing life's treasures and instead offer them back in acknowledgement, or praise.

Today's route along the Kennet is so assiduously fenced and demarcated, we are left in no doubt about who this land belongs to. Knee-height signs have been tapped in every hundred yards to keep potential trespassers on the true way, which is all the provocation I need to wander ever so slightly off, one transgressive foot on private soil. Even the unbounded river has been draped with wire and warnings, while the waters flow chuckling beneath. I'm with them.

Human territoriality, wrote Robert Sack (in his classic study of the theme), is a strategy for shaping behaviour by determining access – in other words, it's about the control of people rather than the land itself. And while not all delimited places are territorial, they become so when their boundaries are employed to indicate access to rights or resources – a school catchment area, for example, or parochial boundary for the reading of marriage banns. Sack contends that the Christian Church adopted territorial organization at quite an early stage: by around AD 300 it had, he suggests, ceased to operate as a human community simply residing in a place, rather as one whose authority structures and organization were explicitly linked to territory – bishops, for example, being increasingly referred to as bishop 'of' a particular locale. His thesis is that territoriality is a means of reifying power (which otherwise can be fairly intangible) and of displacing attention from the human relationship to the territory itself – as in 'the law of the land'.

Territory is, by this token, a social construct that exploits the land in the service of political or religious authority. It makes for a compelling – if incomplete – case and one that is recognizable in the English Church from its inception. The parish system that washed ashore on the Kent coast with St Augustine gave an undeniably territorial basis for church organization that remains largely, if precariously, intact in the present day. Blackstone's *Commentaries on the Laws of England* describes a parish as 'that circuit of ground in which the souls under the care of one parson or vicar do inhabit'.[47] All of the rights (or 'rectory') associated with this – the payment of tithes, in particular – reinforced the identification of local churches with the soil itself.

The benefits of that legacy should not be ignored – foremost among them the assumption that all who reside in a particular place (of whatever faith or persuasion) are parishioners, deserving of the church's care and service. Local welfare simply could not have operated for most of this country's history without such a foundation. Yet it also established the clergy as effective landlords, whose rights of income from their patch (and that of landowners to appoint clergy as patrons to each living) remain evident still, snagging unsuspecting house buyers on the vestigial barbs of chancel repairs.

Being so closely allied to property and the legal appurtenances that followed, Anglican territoriality urgently needs understanding and redefining, or else risks being debased by the paradox that is the established Church's declining secular authority and increasingly secular imagination. We might start by affirming that it is not merely a social or legislative construct, but a theological one, grounded in the gift and promise of land and (given that we are muddy as the dust to which we shall return) our utter dependence on it. The threefold relationship between God, place and people is what makes the church local, and so new financial models must focus not only on congregational giving, but a refreshed appreciation of 'benefice' – the gift of this particular plot. Parish boundaries, likewise, should not be patrolled defensively but viewed as a frame through which to better see and share that treasure. The art is always in the cropping, but the scene is never ours alone.

In Foxbury Copse

The earth has been in a cold kiln overnight. Along the path to the West Woods, the mud clots hard and gives a rough crumble topping to the fields. Furred this morning with a light snowfall, a few minute flakes still bob about like midges, or dust motes.

These thousand acres are an exiled section of the Savernake Forest, which once extended its shade right across this corner of the county. Unlike the twisted oaks of the Savernake, however, the West Woods have leaner lines, harvested when the Forestry Commission took control in the 1930s. Mostly planted to beech and conifer, the view here in winter is striking, striated – a bar chart of sheer vertical growth. I trudge among the adolescent trees, feeling a twinge in my joints.

In July last year, the West Woods were raised from anonymity by being declared as the original location for the sarsen megaliths of Stonehenge. The extraction of these easily workable rocks continued here until 1939 and the advent of cheap concrete, thus ending a 5,000-year-old industry. There are repairs to Windsor Castle and kerbstones in Swindon that employ West Woods sarsens, and they still rubble its surface. One or two are stood upright – a transfiguration that sets them apart, to pique archaeological interest.

The Wansdyke cuts through here also, like the seams of an old wound. Exploring the eastern boundary known as Foxbury Copse, I found myself standing inside it a couple of days ago. Between the lips of a leafy ditch I was, I realized, on the verge of two kingdoms whose ancient division we still don't understand. Romano-British or Anglo-

Saxon, the Wansdyke is a phantom boundary, which one can walk straight through, without resistance.

To remain serviceable, borders need continual maintenance: every untended rivalry will soften over time unless we continue to dig. Because nature has a way of rounding the ridges, performing its natural bridgework of decomposition, we must allow the land to do its job. Being fissiparous and self-obsessed, we forget that it is the essential unifying thing – not only in a universal sense, but in the real particularities of local belonging. What eventually brings peace between warring tribes is either their weariness with conflict, or – more durably – a narrative that recognizes common ground. No lasting culture can grow without that footing.

'To be rooted', wrote Simone Weil (after her country had been felled by the Nazis in 1940), 'is perhaps the most important and least recognized need of the human soul.'[48] And the growing of roots, she went on to explore, demands that people find a good way of loving the land: of reckoning with patriotism, in other words – not as a monolithic thing, manipulated by the state ('a cold concern, which cannot inspire love') but the organic local affection that grows as easily as a self-seeded sapling.

Fascism mechanized this loyalty, pressing it into terrible national service. Yet for all its blood-and-soil posturing, the myth that we are bound first by ethnicity is a peculiarly rootless creed. Peculiarly modern, too, for the arrogance of modernity was to override local attachment and assume that space–time could be conquered in abstract. Britons in their imperial phase were especially prone to this conceit, whereby the remote scoring of lines on supposedly uncharted territory was still wreaking its chaotic voodoo across the globe generations after.

Every technological advance is, in some way, a manipulation of space – the written word included. As Weil observed in *The Need for Roots*: 'One cannot cut out from the continuity of space and time an event as it were like an atom; but the inadequacy of human language obliges one to talk as though one could.' Our current identity-based divisions are so sharply fragmented in part because we cannot (yet, perhaps) cope with social media's extreme dislocation. Any mosaic we form from the shards of digital culture must ease them – and us – back into place.

The Wansdyke peters out at the fringe of the West Woods, whose highest branches shiver and creak in leafless percussion. Through the snow-sequinned air above them circles an all-surveying buzzard, suspended like a mobile.

Epilogue

Snap

The village of Snap no longer exists, but is helpfully sign-posted, nonetheless. Lost settlements are not always so easily found as this, and a brisk five-minute stroll from the Aldbourne Road and I am at the site, marked in gothic script on my map. There are several of these invisible communities on the Marlborough Downs and lately I have become keen to pay each a pastoral visit, scanning them for signs of life. Unlike the previous one (Shaw, on the periphery of the West Woods, whose medieval residents are evidenced only by an occasional lumpy ridge in the grass), Snap satisfies by having been inhabited almost within living memory. Always a small place, by 1909 just two villagers remained, and most buildings were destroyed when the area was used for military training during World War One.

May days arrive early, beautifully prepared – and this morning's virginal sky has been ready for some time, like the well-rehearsed birds and breakfasting cattle who glance up as I bustle in, late to the gathering. Situated within a grove of youngish trees, Snap seems at first to have completely gone, until squared lines of rubble emerge amid the greenery, and a series of homesteads becomes noticeable. Standing in one of these chambers of the human hearth cannot but feel intrusive, causing one to wonder whether time is porous enough to be haunted in reverse.

An abandoned settlement easily calls to our imagination, for it speaks of a belonging that is familiar and concrete but just out of reach. These vacant bricks could house whatever we want them to, whereas our dwellings are more or less fixed, moulds to which we must accommodate. Every such place is also a parable – a prophetic sign, even – and the story of Snap is no different. Its sacrifice to the profits of sheep farming offers a final, passing shot of a countryside transformed by enclosures of land and the cloth industry that burgeoned alongside the rearing of vast flocks. At one point, the Bishop of Winchester alone owned 30,000 sheep on Salisbury Plain.

Parish churches, engrossed and gilded beyond all possible need of their community, were a regular beneficiary of those made wealthy by the wool trade, although none was built here. Snap's witness to the golden fleece was its own demise. Two large farms, which together had provided villagers' employment, were left untenanted by the agricultural depression afflicting late-Victorian Britain and bought up by a butcher from nearby Ramsbury, John Wilson, who converted them into a sheep run and thus forced the remaining villagers' departure. It was an episode that provoked great controversy, even leading to the local MP being sued for describing the Wilson family as oppressive and tyrannical. An account from the 1960s, however, found this outrage already overgrown with other myths of desertion, locals supposing it had to do with their water supply.

As the landscape historian Richard Muir observed in his study of Britain's lost villages, if such a lapse of memory can take place within fifty years, it is little surprise that the undocumented lives of earlier generations of dispossessed poor are as obscure to us as forgotten walls under the soil. At precisely the point when Snap was in terminal decline, that hidden culture was becoming a focus of liberal intellectual concern, especially among those who sought to recover the lore, language and artistic expression of rural communities. The English folk revival – with its Maypoles, Morris dancers and other approximations of Merrie England – was one of the great social and educational projects of the twentieth century and a monumental act of historical invention. Its narrative of extinction and retrieval was necessary in order to fill a perceived void among the modern, industrialized masses – namely, the meaningful ties and traditions of a small rustic community. The only lost things we tend to seek are those we miss in the present.

Collection and circulation of folk songs by Cecil Sharp and others became a particular totem: half-recalled snatches of a 'national music' grounded (according to Ralph Vaughan Williams) in a mystic parochialism. Folk song should, Vaughan Williams felt, enable people to 'feel at home', so he set about rechristening these tunes and placing them at the heart of the parish: within the leaf-green covers of *The English Hymnal*, whose first edition appeared in 1906. Through ongoing presence in Anglican churches and schools (the latter via its companion volume for children, *Songs of Praise*), *The English Hymnal* ensured that Christian worship became a most effective carrier of the folk revival, long after its ideological binding had foxed and faded.

While its aims – national and spiritual unity, deepening of local roots – were lofty and, to a degree, laudable, they presumed upon a 'lost' class of peasantry, untainted by mechanized culture, who were on the verge of dying out. As Georgina Boyes explored in *The Imagined Village*, her interrogation of the movement, this assumption was simply not borne out by its own fieldwork. The 'Folk' were essentially a construct, who needed to exist and so did – allowing the gatekeepers of the folk revival to decide which among their values and traditions were legitimate in order to further their missionary ends.

Social and political movements are prone to doing this, of course (as is the Church whenever it presumes to know the mind of Christ), but their authority ceases in the moment they instrumentalize those they represent – or become remote from them, which is the usual counterpart.

When it becomes ideologically necessary for a certain group of people to act or think a certain way – the 'white working class', say – contact with reality soon disappears.

Frustrating though it can be to our causes, communal identity (past and present) is usually far more open and harder to categorize than we might imagine or need it to be, and is under continual renegotiation. The English village – a compact of ideal and reality – is peculiarly susceptible to being conscripted in ways that limit its potential, like the assumption it ought only to grow by a process of faithful reproduction, as if it were a photograph, captured by time and unable to move. Unlike the fluid and mutable urban scene, the village must advance in freeze-frame: tracked by facsimiles of what was never static to begin with.

In 1946, Penguin Books published *The Anatomy of the Village*: an unusual manifesto for renewing rural life as the postwar era began, written by the eminent planner Thomas Sharp.[49] In this lucidly written and (given the crimes of planning about to be committed on many provincial towns) surprisingly balanced report, Sharp notes how 'Something of a romantic fallacy has grown up round the idea of building in the country', warning of the danger of 'tradition gone morbid'. Respect for heritage was vital, but only if it really did offer life and growth, adding with emphasis: 'A true tradition ... is not a pool which has welled-up at some particular moment of time, and has remained stagnant ever since.' Sharp's conclusion was that 'simplicity' of style and scale is the village's defining character, which is perhaps why they lend themselves so readily to possession – and dispossession. Small communities are more stoutly defended because we who inhabit such places see them more immediately as 'ours': you can throw your arms around a village, and never let go.

They also retain a tenacious national significance, even when the vast majority of us no longer live in one. At home I am reading Ayisha Malik's novel *This Green and Pleasant Land*,[50] in which Bilal, a cultural Muslim living in the pregnantly named village of Babbel's End, seeks to enact his mother's dying request that he build there a mosque and so recover his own inheritance of faith. It proves infinitely more provocative to start a mosque in Babbel's End than in Birmingham. The very word is 'hissed in the village hall' as Bilal makes his proposal to the parish council, and the ensuing controversy (which involves a suitably conflicted and liberal-minded vicar) centres around contested ideas of both heritage and Englishness, for which the church building offers an intense focus. It is a perceptive and generous-hearted story, which avoids tidy platitudes and finds hope in the patient forming of neighbourly relations – the essence, after all, of the village ethic.

All of which suggests that unless we rebuild the village, we will not rebuild England – or redefine its place within the United Kingdom, within Europe, or our unsettled world. Whatever realm we seek can only be located among people sometimes intolerably different from ourselves, but with whom we share undeniable common ground. England was long ago wedded to Christianity – too long ago, indeed, for that covenant to be claimed only by Anglicans. And just as its narrative once offered resources that proved uniquely advantageous to becoming one people from many, a trace memory of that promise remains, on a half-term holiday named Whitsuntide. Traditionally this is when Christians commemorate the gift of the Holy Spirit, uncorked like spraying prosecco over the internationals gathered in Jerusalem for the Jewish feast of Pentecost. Each one, apparently, was enabled to hear the gospel in their own tongue – and from this riot of translation the early Church was impelled from confinement into the furthest reaches of the ancient world. Not the reversal of Babel, then, but its baptism – a christening, not a flattening, of local particularity.

The Holy Ghost is a wraith from hereafter – breath of life in the face of death. Unlike others, this spirit is *arrabon* – foretaste of what is to come. Walking from Snap, sunlight sprinkled by shimmying leaves, I spot an overgrown stone placed by children from Toothill School in nearby Swindon, in honour of its departed people. Dated 1991, and that school now closed, it marks a memory of a memory, making me idly question whether there might also be signs hereabouts of lost villages as yet unconceived. After all, romances of the future have at least a fair chance of coming true.

Whitsun 2021

References

1 E. M. Forster, *The Longest Journey*, London, Penguin Classics, 2006, p. 126.

2 *Malvern 1941: The Life of the Church and the Order of Society*, London, Longmans, 1941, p. 221.

3 Linda Colley, *Britons: Forging the Nation 1707–1837*, London, Pimlico, 1994, p. 54.

4 Ernest Renan, *What Is a Nation? and Other Political Writings*, New York, Columbia University Press, 2018, p. 261.

5 Richard Helgersen, *Forms of Nationhood: The Elizabethan Writings of England*, Chicago, IL, University of Chicago Press, 1994, p. 1.

6 Sir Walter Raleigh, Thomas Birch and William Oldys, *The History of the World* (1614), Charleston, SC, Nabu Press, 2013, Preface.

7 Michael Foucault, *Discipline and Punish: The Birth of the Prison*, London, Penguin Modern Classics, 2020.

8 Available at https://web.mit.edu/allanmc/www/foucault1.pdf (accessed 24.8.21).

9 W. H. Auden, 'In Memory of W. B. Yeats', *Another Time*, London Random House, 1940.

10 Bruce Dickins and Alan S. C. Ross, eds, *The Dream of the Rood*, London, Methuen's Old English Library, 1963.

11 G. K. Chesterton, 'The Priest of Spring', *Stories, Essays and Poems*, London, Dent, 1935, p. 164.

12 Keith Thomas, *Man and the Natural World: Changing Attitudes in England 1500–1800*, London, Penguin, 1991; and *Religion and the Decline of Magic: Studies in Popular Beliefs in Sixteenth and Seventeenth-Century England*, London, Penguin, 2003.

13 Ralph Waldo Emerson, *Compensation, Self-Reliance, And Other Essays*, CreateSpace Independent Publishing Platform, 2016.

14 Dietrich Bonhoeffer, *Letters and Papers from Prison*, London, Fontana, 1959, p. 100.

15 Wendell Berry, 'The Work of Local Culture', the 1988 Iowa Humanities Lecture, Iowa Humanities Board, 1988.

16 Thomas Fuller, *Mixt contemplations in better times by Thomas Fuller ... (1660)*, Early English Books Online (EEBO) on the ProQuest Platform, 2011.

17 William Cobbett, *Rural Rides*, London, Penguin Classics, 2001, p. 296; emphasis original.

18 Nicola Whyte, *Inhabiting the Landscape: Place, Custom and Memory, 1500-1800*, Kindle edn, Macclesfield, Windgather Press, 2009.

19 Aldous Huxley, *The Doors of Perception and Heaven and Hell*, New York, HarperCollins, p. 134.

20 Dorothy L. Sayers, *The Mind of the Maker*, London, Methuen, 1941, pp. 17, 19.

21 George Herbert, 'The Flower', *The Temple*, London, Penguin Classics, 2017.

22 Peter Hunter Blair, *An Introduction to Anglo-Saxon England*, Cambridge, Cambridge University Press, 1977, p. 146.

23 Henry of Huntingdon, *The History of the English People 1000–1154*, Diana Greenway, trans., Oxford: Oxford World's Classics, 1996, 2002, pp. 17–18.

24 Richard Jefferies, *The Story of My Heart: My Autobiography*, London, Longmans, Green & Co., 1883, pp. 5–6, 43, 108.

25 Alfred Williams, *Poems in Wiltshire*, London, Erskine Mac-Donald, 1911.

26 Andrew Motion, *The Cinder Path*, London, Faber & Faber, 2010, p. 57.

27 Hilaire Belloc, *The Old Road*, London, Constable, 1911, p. 7.

28 Richard M. Gale (ed.), *The Philosophy of Time: A Collection of Essays*, London, Macmillan, 1968, p. 365.

29 Patrick Wormald, *The First Code of English Law*, Canterbury, Canterbury Commemoration Society, 2005, p. 19.

30 Simon Keynes and Michael Lapidge, trans., *Alfred the Great: Asser's Life of King Alfred and Other Contemporary Sources*, London, Penguin Classics, 1983, pp. 163–4.

31 Louisa Adjoa Parker, *Dorset's Hidden Histories: Beginning to Explore Four Hundred Years of the Presence of Black People in Dorset*, Ferndown, Dorset, Deed, 2007.

32 Robert Wedderburn, *The Horrors of Slavery and Other Writings*, Princeton, NJ, Markus Wiener, 1991.

33 Available at https://www.churchofengland.org/sites/default/files/2021-04/FromLamentToAction-report.pdf (accessed 25.8.21).

34 William Blake, *The Complete Poetry and Prose of William Blake*, David V. Erdman, ed., Berkeley, CA, University of California Press, 1982, pp. 702–3.

35 Julian Barnes, *England, England*, London, Jonathan Cape, 1998, p. 237.

36 Gerrard Winstanley, *The Law of Freedom and Other Writings*, Christopher Hill, ed., Harmondsworth, Penguin, 1973, p. 148.

37 Patrick Wright, *The Village That Died for England*, London, Jonathan Cape Ltd, 1995, p. 41.

38 John Coffey, *Persecution and Toleration in Protestant England 1558–1689*, London, Routledge, 2000.

39 William Temple, *Christianity and Social Order*, London, SCM Press, 1950, pp. 63–4.

40 Patrick Wright, *On Living in an Old Country*, Oxford, Oxford University Press, 2009, p. 65.

41 Mary Douglas, *Purity and Danger*, London, Routledge, 2002.

42 Lecture available at https://ires.ubc.ca/mark-carneys-reith-lectures-on-financial-systems-climate-change/ (accessed 25.8.21).

43 Peter Laslett, *The World We Have Lost*, London, Routledge, 2021, p. 234.

44 R. H. Tawney, *Religion and the Rise of Capitalism*, London, Verso Books, 2015, p. 273.

45 Richard Jefferies, *Wood Magic*, London, Cassell, Petter, Galpin & Co., 1881, pp. 211–12; *The Story of My Heart*, p. 61.

46 George Herbert, 'Providence', *The Complete English Poems*, London, Penguin Classics, 2004.

47 *Blackstone's Commentaries on the Laws of England*, Wayne Morrison, ed., 4 vols, London, Routledge-Cavendish, 2001.

48 Simone Weil, *The Need for Roots: Prelude to a Declaration of Duties Towards Mankind*, London, Routledge, 1952, p. 41.

49 Thomas Sharp, *The Anatomy of the Village*, London, Penguin, 1946, 2017, pp. 5, 66.

50 Ayisha Malik, *This Green and Pleasant Land*, London, Zaffre, 2019.

Lightning Source UK Ltd.
Milton Keynes UK
UKHW041844211121
394211UK00006B/53/J

9 780334 061144